How Can We Create a Free, Just,
and Sustainable World?

HOW CAN WE CREATE A FREE, JUST, AND SUSTAINABLE WORLD?

A Convoco Edition

CORINNE MICHAELA FLICK (ED.)

Convoco! Editions

The publisher has used its best endeavors to ensure that the URLs for
external websites referred to in this book are correct and active at the
time of going to press. However, the publisher has no responsibility
for the websites and can make no guarantee that a site will remain
live or that the content is or will remain appropriate.

Convoco Foundation
Brienner Strasse 28
D – 80333 Munich
www.convoco.co.uk

British Library Cataloguing-in-Publication data: a catalogue
record for this book is available from the British Library.

Edited by Dr. Corinne Michaela Flick
Translated from German by Philippa Hurd
Layout and typesetting by Jill Sawyer Phypers

ISBN: 978-1-917523-60-8

Previously published Convoco titles:

Is the Open Society Sustainable in Case of Emergency? (2024)

Equality in an Unequal World (2023)

How much Freedom must we Forgo to be Free? (2022)

New Global Alliances: Institutions, Alignments and Legitimacy in the Contemporary World (2021)

The Standing of Europe in the New Imperial World Order (2020)

The Multiple Futures of Capitalism (2019)

The Common Good in the 21st Century (2018)

Authority in Transformation (2017)

Power and its Paradoxes (2016)

To Do or Not To Do—Inaction as a Form of Action (2015)

Dealing with Downturns: Strategies in Uncertain Times (2014) Collective

Law-Breaking—A Threat to Liberty (2013)

no now without then, no there
without here, finally
you glimpse the truth of it:
    that we are bound to relation
    that we are *we* inescapably

Victoria Adukwei Bulley

CONTENTS

INTRODUCTION

Dear Friends of Convoco,

"How can we create a free, just, and sustainable world?" Given today's ever-increasing pace of change, this is perhaps *the* key question. It consists of two parts: what makes a free, just, and sustainable world, and how can we create and preserve it? The question combines thoughts about the common good, freedom, and equality, as well as strategic considerations. Above all this, there is ever-increasing uncertainty. The question now must be about how we can effect results in practice, because the time for appeals and statements of intent is over.

How does the world present itself at the start of the 21st century? From a geopolitical perspective, today's world is the result of the collapse of the Soviet Union, which has not only disrupted the stability of the East, but the stability of the West has also developed fault lines. This loss of stability goes hand in hand with China's economic rise and the Global South's political strengthening. Hence, we find ourselves in a new period of competition and an age of increased dependencies, not to mention transnational challenges such as climate change.

Initially, these transnational challenges were thought likely to unite the world. But it's now clear that they are more likely to divide it. For example, the Global South's perspective on climate change differs profoundly from that of the North.

Naturally, various opinions exist as to which factors fundamentally make up a free, just, and sustainable world. It is undisputed that two essential factors are peace, meaning stability, and a healthy environment. These are the cornerstones which are most clearly under threat, and they are also interdependent. Today, a third new aspect needs to be added to these two significant areas: We must meet the challenge posed by technology in the form of Artificial Intelligence. AI is not some kind of cure-all that will save humankind. It can only be part of a free, just, and sustainable world if we use it in such a way that it serves as a tool for humanity. So we must learn "to work in concert with AI." Additionally, we must create governance structures that can guide development and strategically align it with the objectives of attaining a free, just, and sustainable world.

Peace, a healthy environment, and technology that serves humankind—together, these three topics form the foundations of the discussions offered in this book about what a free, just, and sustainable world might be. Of course, these three adjectives are only examples; they are not exhaustive. Above all, this list should be expanded to include the terms open, prosperous, and secure. Access to water, food, education, energy, and—not forgetting—the safe exercise of the right to vote are also of utmost importance for implementing these objectives.

Achieving these goals has been an aim for public-spirited citizens for many decades. Throughout history, there have always been attempts to improve the world and establish a more ideal society. There is a long tradition here, which, if you look at Europe and the Enlightenment, began with Denis Diderot and his *Encyclopedia* in the 18th century. He attempted to collect the world's knowledge and make it accessible to his fellow Europeans. In doing so, he hoped to make the world more free, just, and (although the term had not yet been coined) something close to sustainable. But as the proverb, going back to Bernard of Clairvaux in the 12th century, states: "The road to hell is paved with good intentions." The French Revolution wanted to improve human coexistence through liberty, equality, and fraternity, but it ended in the horrors of the Terror. It was followed in 1804 by Napoleon's *Code Civil*, which tried to enforce equality and liberty using the law in what was ultimately an unfree, authoritarian state. In Germany, it was the 1848 Revolution leading to the Frankfurt Constitution, meaning the Constitution of St. Paul's Church, which provided another model. In the 20th century, the Russian Revolution of 1917 was supposed to bring about significant societal change. We all know how that ended. The inhuman ideologies of Communism and National Socialism represent attempts to create a different and "ideal" society, but brought physical and moral destruction instead.

All these approaches show that wanting to change the world is easier than actually changing it, and changing it for the better is more difficult still. Unfortunately, even today we have to face the truth that the Green Transformation is finding it very hard to get off the ground, that opinions on how to deal with Artificial Intelligence differ worldwide, and that views of what constitutes a good life sharply diverge.

So what conclusion should we draw? What do we need to acknowledge?

Every individual exists solely within relationships. I exist only through my relationship with others. And these others also include nature. Today, more than ever, it is essential to embrace this understanding. It is about acknowledging the laws set by nature—the laws of physics, biochemistry, and the social sciences—and living in accord with them. The role of science is to demonstrate these laws. Only then can human existence be guaranteed, and we can create a free, just, and sustainable world.

Convoco can look back on twenty years of mutual exchange. Together, let us build a bridge to the future.

Corinne Michaela Flick, March 2025

THESES

GABRIEL FELBERMAYR

In order for the world to remain free, just, and sustainable for as many people as possible, difficult distribution problems will have to be solved. To ensure that the risks that already exist do not continue to grow and, if they do occur, lead to devastating consequences, investments are necessary to contain the risks and to mitigate the damage if risks materialize. This involves *ex ante* and *ex post* measures, i.e. before a crisis occurs and afterwards.

MORITZ SCHULARICK

The way forward requires a rebuilding of the state's capacities to govern. This includes investments in education, effective governance, and global cooperation. But implementing these goals in polarized political environments and in the face of global uncertainty is a Herculean task.

PHILIPP PATTBERG

To make global governance fit for purpose, I suggest five areas of reform: inclusive decision-making, future-orientation, rights of nature, adapting for breakdown, and realizing the nexus approach.

CHRISTINE LANGENFELD

Dealing with climate change poses a challenge to constitutional democracy. However, climate protection can only be achieved using constitutional means. In Germany, but in other countries too, strengthening constitutional democracies that can withstand the temptation of populism is a precondition for tackling climate change successfully.

CLAUDIA WIESNER

When seen in relation to the Anthropocene condition, the crisis symptoms and challenges not only reveal a crisis of democracy, but a crisis of modernity and modern thinking altogether. This diagnosis is far from being just a philosophical one: it has very concrete and material consequences.

CLEMENS FUEST

If we understand the concept of the social market economy not as a number of fixed principles but as a policy style, it has a lot to offer as a framework for economic policy of the future.

MARTIN KORTE

Preserving biodiversity and making necessary changes in behavior in response to climate change are particularly hard at all systemic levels—politics, the economy, society, and each individual—because our brains tend to perceive what we expect to think and do out of habit and, when changes occur, place greater importance on the loss than on the possible gain. In doing so, we perceive our future self as a stranger, which leads us to not relating the consequences of our actions to ourselves.

STEFAN KORIOTH

Every state, every institution, every individual must be held accountable for their own actions that damage the climate—and must come up with alternatives. Those who cause climate damage should pay for the elimination of such damage or compensate for it. Democratic and market-based structures are the most compatible with a consistent implementation of this principle.

BIRKE HÄCKER

The rapid advance of digitalization presents new regulatory challenges. Europe regards itself as pioneering this field and has already introduced various regulatory frameworks; yet the importance of "digital inclusion" is often overlooked.

HANS-DIETER LUCAS

Europe needs to considerably improve its decision mechanisms and its military capabilities. That will require increased defense spending and more capable European defense industries. Furthermore, Europe needs a new mindset based on the recognition that its security will be challenged in many ways for the foreseeable future. It will need resilience as well as unity.

TIMO MEYNHARDT

Common sense is a source of practical reason that makes an individual's inner voice heard and encourages us to trust our intuition. It cannot replace a lack of factual knowledge, but it can close relevant gaps and guide our actions. The wealth of experience inherent to common sense should not stop at what "the man on the Clapham omnibus" considers reasonable and thus beneficial to the common good, but should also include the "tree by the side of the road" and the "artificial intelligence around the corner."

HANS ULRICH OBRIST

Like gardens, curating has the power to bring people together. It is also an important part of my work to bring people together. If you want to address the big themes of the 21st century, the challenge is that we need to go beyond the fear of bringing knowledge and the disciplines together.

TINO SEHGAL

One way to see modernity is as an experiment in separation. Growing up in an environment focused on material production, I became much more interested in working with the living and seeing how I can transform situations and people's interactions.

PIET OUDOLF

When you enter a garden, you think it looks wild, but it's organized and composed. That is also why I like to work on public projects and in bigger cities. You connect people with something they probably have inside them but can only work out when they encounter it.

CORINNE M. FLICK

Every individual exists solely within relationships. I exist only through my relationship with others. And these others also include nature. Today, more than ever, it is essential to embrace this understanding. It is about acknowledging the laws set by nature—the laws of physics, biochemistry, and the social sciences—and living in accord with them.

CHAPTER 1

WHAT WOULD A FREE, JUST, AND SUSTAINABLE WORLD LOOK LIKE? IDEAS FROM THE WORLD OF ECONOMICS

GABRIEL FELBERMAYR

INTRODUCTION

What would a free, just, and sustainable world look like, a world in which as many people as possible can live as well as possible? This question is different from the question of a world worth living in, where the mere ability to exist is taken for granted and the focus is more on the conditions for living as "good" a life as possible. The question of a free, just, and sustainable world is radical in the truest sense of the word, because it is about survival and not just the quality of life. Indeed, anthropogenic catastrophes such as uncontrollable climate change, the use of nuclear weapons, or the autonomous development of artificial intelligence threaten the habitability of the Earth for humans.[1]

The question of a free, just, and sustainable world is therefore the question of how catastrophes can be prevented. The question of being free, just, and sustainable therefore seems easier to answer than that of quality of life, because the normative conflict in a binary problem is less than in a fundamentally open issue that is strongly influenced by value judgments. In reality, however, the situation is more complex, because the complete uninhabitability of the Earth for humans is the absolutely extreme—and hopefully very unlikely—scenario, to which one can compare other dramatic but unfortunately completely realistic scenarios in which, while humanity's extinction is not threatened, a dignified life for many people does not seem possible. This short essay will examine which economic institutions and structures we need in the face of these multiple threats, so that as many people as possible can continue to live as well as possible on Earth.

The global challenges of our time are indeed daunting, and they are urgently demanding answers to the question of a free, just, and sustainable world. Climate change poses an existential threat in some regions of our Earth, because cities will become uninhabitable without expensive adaptation and once fertile agricultural land will become unusable.[2] Supporters of "Extinction Rebellion" even fear that climate change could render the whole world uninhabitable. Wars make habitats uninhabitable and threaten the physical existence of hundreds of thousands of people; a nuclear war could devastate the entire Earth. In Ukraine, it is possible that over a million people have died or become disabled as a result of military action.[3] The recent pandemic has shown that, despite all our progress in medicine, humanity is not protected from new diseases—the COVID-19 crisis has probably cost the lives of more than 15 million people worldwide.[4] And technological upheavals, most notably in artificial intelligence, are perceived as a threat to existence.[5] The threats mentioned may be local or global in nature, they can affect the existence of individual groups or that of humanity as a whole. Tipping points play a decisive role, especially in the most extreme scenarios.

If these are exceeded, there is no turning back and the dynamics of the system can no longer be controlled.

But this essay should not just focus on such thoroughly dystopian ideas, because it seems more realistic to assume that while the examples mentioned undermine the living conditions of large parts of the population, they do not make the world uninhabitable per se. If that is the case, then all of these threats—whether they are climatic, military, affecting health or technology—touch on issues of distribution. This means that they have a central economic dimension. It is about resources to adapt to new conditions, about the economic conditions for lasting peace, and about economic structures for governing new technologies. These, in turn, can be determined by political policy. Conversely, the threat to or even destruction of livelihoods can be prevented by establishing the right framework conditions.

EXTINCTION
NUCLEAR WAR

A nuclear war, a climate catastrophe, a deadly virus, technological changes, a meteorite impact—all these can be so devastating as to render human life impossible. When we consider human-made catastrophes, we can always hope that there are ways to prevent them. However, there are no guarantees, because nonlinearities and fundamental problems of coordination can become uncontrollable.

Nuclear warfare could make human life on Earth very difficult or impossible. Game theory research and the wider public domain have been dealing with this issue since the development of the atomic bomb. Nuclear deterrence can ensure peace, even if there are no formal coordination mechanisms between highly armed countries. But there is no guarantee that this strategy will work in all conceivable cases. There is a risk that a nuclear war could escalate due to a miscalculation by one actor.[6] To keep this possibility as low as possible, it is necessary that all parties are as well informed as possible; ideally, a minimum level of information exchange takes place, for example in international forums such as the Organization for Security and Cooperation in Europe. But in the absence of a global regulatory power with the ability to take action, it is not inconceivable that a conflict that might have devastating consequences and thus ultimately harm all participants rather than create a negotiated solution might not escalate. The outbreak of World War I is one example of this.

MODERN MALTHUSIANISM

There is an old line of research in economics that is associated with the English economist Thomas Robert Malthus (1766–1834). In Malthus's reasoning, exponential population growth coupled with linear progress in agricultural productivity leads to recurring famines. The modern incarnation of this fundamental idea can be found in the literature on the limits to growth, as advocated by the Club of Rome, and which is addressed in the de-growth debate.[7] This does not entail the danger of complete self-extinction, but rather the risk of a cyclical development in which humanity repeatedly suffers setbacks. Economic history since 1750 also shows that regional and now global population dynamics are unlikely to be exponential, but rather are logistical,[8] and that productivity development is not linear, but also logistical (with a positive trend). This gives us hope.

More recent literature describes environmental crises that are characterized by rapid and largely unexpected changes in environmental quality that are difficult or impossible to reverse. Examples of this are cases in which certain species have become extinct or an ecosystem has significantly deteriorated. There are typically three prerequisites for a crisis: (i) a failure of governance, (ii) an ecological system that has reached a tipping point, and (iii) an interaction between the economy and the environment with positive feedback. To illustrate these conditions, Scott Taylor[9] has developed a simple model that shows how a crisis can arise. He draws on information about past and present crises to illustrate the mechanisms involved quantitatively as well. This model can be used, for example, to usefully analyze under which conditions climate change actually represents an impending crisis.

In a famous essay on the rise and fall of the Easter Island civilization, James Brander and Scott Taylor[10] showed that Malthusian logic can also lead to extinction catastrophes. They propose a model of general equilibrium that models the complex dynamics between renewable resources and the population. They use the predator-prey model used in biology, in which humans are the predator and the resource base is the prey. They apply the model to the case of Easter Island and show that plausible parameter values produce a cyclical adjustment in population and resource stocks. A near-monotonic adjustment arises for higher values of a resource regeneration parameter, as might apply elsewhere in Polynesia, resulting in complete decline. The authors also describe other civilizations that might have declined due to population overshooting and endogenous resource degradation.

A fundamental problem in modern Malthusianism is the failure of political coordination. For various reasons, the price system does not internalize the upcoming shortage and impending catastrophe, and private actors pursue their behavior beyond a tipping point, making any subsequent correction impossible. A robust political coordination mechanism is therefore needed to curb the unsustainable consumption of resources. Ultimately, this is about solving a distribution problem, because (according to the model) every individual involved tries to avoid cutting back on the consumption they need for survival, while making other actors shoulder the burden of cutbacks.

This problem is reminiscent of the climate issue, in which avoiding a climate catastrophe also requires a global reduction in greenhouse gas emissions, with individual actors or governments having very little incentive to forego emissions and thus suffer short-term cutbacks in consumption. Even if people solemnly vow to reduce emissions, there is a great temptation at the individual level to abandon one's promises. And this becomes all the greater the more it is expected that other actors will also succumb to the same temptation. At a regional or national level, one can imagine that a strong and forward-looking state would enforce the measures needed to return to a sustainable path. At a global level, this is very difficult—all the more reason why the fate of Easter Island should serve as a warning.

As in the Malthusian catastrophe scenario, the failure of coordination is exacerbated by a high time preference rate. This means that developments in the future are given little weight in actors' present-day decisions. There is a lot of evidence for this at the individual level.[11] But even beyond the individual level, for example between generations, possible events impacting the future are given little weight in the present. An intense debate has arisen about this in the economic literature on climate policy, which has still not been resolved. One camp uses the time preference rate measurable on the financial markets,[12] while the other side argues that it is unethical to value the welfare of future generations lower than the welfare of the present-day cohort.[13] The majority of current literature tends towards Nicholas Stern's position. Ultimately, this position is also compatible with the classical economic theory of expected utility. If, in an extreme case, the welfare of a future generation were to become negative, then even if the probabilities of occurrence were very low, this would be enough to make the expected utility extremely negative. This then also results in appropriate recommendations for action, that is, to combat climate change very decisively now, even at great cost. However, enforcing this politically remains an enormous hurdle, because scientific insights are by no means enough to be decisive factors in democratic elections. In addition, the latest evidence shows that the excessive underestimation of future benefits is even more pronounced in complex decision-making problems.[14] This applies to global warming caused by anthropogenic processes, but also to other processes that are associated with high returns today and high risks in the future, such as artificial intelligence.

ARTIFICIAL INTELLIGENCE

Similar questions arise in the context of the development of artificial intelligence (AI). Charles Jones[15] follows a recent large body of literature arguing that advances in AI are a double-edged sword.[16] On the one hand, such advances can boost economic growth because AI increases our ability to innovate. On the other hand, many experts fear that these advances pose an existential risk: The creation of a superintelligence that does not reflect human values could lead to catastrophic results, possibly even the extinction of humanity. In his work, Jones deals with the optimal use of AI technology in light of these opportunities and risks. Under what conditions should we pursue the rapid progress of AI, and under what conditions should we stop?

If it is probable that the use of AI will lead to a catastrophe for humanity, then its development can be seen as a lottery in which a catastrophic "draw" is possible in the future. The answer to the question of whether to ban this dangerous lottery depends fundamentally on how individuals and society conceive of risk and time preference. It is therefore extremely important to develop a good understanding of these attitudes and measure them empirically. The latter is difficult, perhaps impossible, so the focus must be on making investments that will make AI as safe as possible. And the appropriate regulation is needed, but this requires coordination between individual countries.

EXTREME CRISES AND SHORTAGES
DISTRIBUTION PROBLEMS

Our discussion so far has dealt with scenarios that might lead to a complete collapse of human civilization.

In this respect, the scenarios are certainly extreme and unlikely, but they are not impossible and must therefore be taken seriously. But even if climate change, armed conflicts, or technological risks do not lead to global catastrophes, they are still capable of causing temporary, extreme shortages of essential consumer goods—food, usable living space, or energy. Dealing with such shortages efficiently is a truly economic problem. In this context, issues of distribution cannot be ignored either, because market processes are not enough to deal with extreme crises of scarcity. If both the supply and demand for goods are not very price-sensitive, then adverse supply shocks can lead to market-clearing prices that are simply unaffordable for many people. This problem became apparent in Europe during the 2022/23 energy crisis, when market prices for natural gas rose to 340 euros per megawatt hour over the short term, after being below 30 euros for decades. In such a situation, it is highly likely that market processes will collapse, for example because they are being politically undermined, which then leads to rationing, i.e. an administrative allocation of goods. We would expect this to affect essential food products as well. However, rationing would be a highly political approach.

These ideas chime well with the ideas proposed by Nobel prizewinner Amartya Sen in his famous 1983 book *Poverty and Famines: An Essay on Entitlement and Deprivation*.[17] In this book Sen showed that food shortages do not necessarily lead to famine, but that they are due to a failure of the political-economic system. He argues that democracy prevents famines because it gives rights to all people and thus an adequate distribution of food ensures the survival of all members of a population despite shortages. Such distribution can indeed include rationing, but it is of the utmost importance that rationing is carried out as efficiently as possible (i.e. without creating wastage) and that the mechanisms used are generally accepted and perceived as fair. Rationing that does not meet these criteria runs the risk of encouraging the development of black markets, which can then lead to the reduction of demand among people on lower incomes.

In order to be able to deal as well as possible with extreme crises that can cause massive shortages and to maintain the living conditions of as many people as possible, we need, in economic language, appropriate mechanisms that must be developed before a crisis occurs. On the one hand, this involves *ex ante* measures that make the occurrence of crises less likely and ensure greater resilience in the face of crises, and on the other hand, *ex post* mechanisms that take effect when a crisis has already occurred. Here we will focus primarily on preventive measures; as we have already indicated, dealing with crises that have already occurred happens outside of market processes and requires advance planning that can be activated at short notice.

WHAT ARE CRITICAL GOODS?

In all cases, however, the question arises as to which products or services require special provisions. What indeed are critical goods? If such goods are not available, even in the short term, there is a risk of serious harm to life and limb. The debate in the wake of the COVID-19 crisis, the subsequent supply chain disruptions, and the geopolitical risks that are now at the heart of the debate has shown that the definition of such goods depends on the context. In a work I co-authored with Eckhard Janeba,[18] for example, we recently pointed this out. In a work I co-authored with Martin Braml,[19] we proposed a conceptually simple test that can be used to identify critical goods. Goods can only be described as critical, in the sense of the need for state intervention, only if three criteria are met simultaneously. First, the goods must be of a kind for which there are no short-term substitutes such as comparable products or alternative sources of supply. Second, the goods are directly consumer-related, and their absence would lead to hunger, illness, or other danger to life. This means that critical goods are typically consumer goods; capital goods (such as photovoltaic cells) are only critical goods if they have a direct impact on the population's supply (PV cells do not). And third, the market must have failed, because only then can state intervention lead to better results. This is extremely important because a state crisis response reduces private incentives to invest in an individual's own crisis resilience, for example by taking out private insurance or promoting the diversification of sources of supply. The state should only intervene if the actions of private entities systematically lead to inefficiently high risk-taking in society.

In many cases, households and companies have the option of taking out insurance against the effects of crises that may happen, for example against storm damage. This is more difficult in crisis scenarios that affect entire countries and industries. In addition to taking out insurance policies, there is the option of diversification. Both measures incur costs; however, the advantages of greater crisis resilience are often social in nature, because when individual companies make decisions, for example, the effects on product diversity or on other companies in the production network are not internalized, in this case leading to insufficient diversification.

ECONOMIC POLICY MEASURES

When the above-mentioned criteria (1) to (3) are met simultaneously, this becomes a job for economic policy. Effective measures should be applied to the Single Market as a whole and not just to individual countries. And they should operate in the event of various kinds of shocks—extreme weather events, military disruptions, or technological crises. In Felbermayr and Janeba[20] we discuss a whole list of possible measures. Here we will only refer to the most important ones, which are intended to operate *ex ante* to prevent situations arising due to shocks that could massively affect the living conditions of regions and people.

The excessive concentration of supply chains in just a few countries could be combated in a targeted manner using special quota tariffs. This means tariffs on imports of raw materials or intermediate products from countries whose share in the supply market exceed a certain percentage. If imports from such countries become more expensive, companies have an incentive to access sources from other countries or to substitute the respective product with other products. For example, in the future the EU could stipulate that liquefied or pipeline gas can be imported duty-free from countries whose share of total imports into the EU does not exceed a certain percentage threshold. In order to avoid the need for additional Member-country-specific quota tariffs, which would be incompatible with the principles of the European customs union, such a policy would have to be accompanied by an expansion of the European internal distribution infrastructure. The aim would be for EU imports to be both duty-free and sufficiently diversified. Whether such a quota tariff is compatible with WTO law is likely to be controversial. However, it is clear that similar structures already exist in agricultural trade. Such an instrument would probably also find support among many poorer countries, such as India.

Where countries still have external tariffs on inter-mediate products or raw materials, they can vary these within the framework agreed under WTO law, i.e. without discriminating against trading partners. For example, there are tariffs on lithium and gallium, on many steel products and other metals. Tariff barriers are still particularly strong in the agricultural sector. These tariffs could be adjusted to suit the situation: When world market prices are high, they could be reduced; when world market prices are low, import tariffs could be raised to the maximum rate compliant with WTO regulations. Switzerland operates such a system of "breathing tariffs," which should also be helpful for many poorer countries. Admittedly, this cannot directly incentivize diversification because the system would have to be applied equally to all trading partners. However, it could mitigate the impact of shortages on prices. It could also provide incentives to develop alternatives to the imported goods in question.

In order for companies to diversify, they need the best and least bureaucratic access to as many international procurement markets as possible. This means minimizing import tariffs or non-tariff restrictions on trade. Today's increasingly protectionist policies, which are justified with the aim of ensuring security of supply, is not a solution—in fact the exact opposite. The more isolated countries are, the harder they are impacted by catastrophes that occur within their own borders. However, the trade policy of most countries needs a strategic shift: Instead of focusing primarily on opening up new sales markets for their own goods and services, the strategic goal of securing supply in their own economy must become increasingly important. This means, among other things, making agreements that create legal certainty in the procurement of raw materials, for importers as well as for producer countries.

INVESTMENTS TO IMPROVE SECURITY OF SUPPLY

In many cases it is not possible to diversify the procurement base because there are only a few countries that mine certain raw materials, or because production capacities are limited. It can therefore make sense for companies from other countries to invest in regions rich in raw materials in order to find alternative sources of supply. Because legal certainty is often not sufficiently guaranteed in these countries, in the past investment promotion and protection treaties (IPT) have been entered into. These have fallen into disrepute since the debate about TTIP, the transatlantic free trade agreement. Such fundamental criticism cannot be objectively justified, because the treaties address the very real problem that German or European investments in third countries are exposed to a political risk against which investors cannot defend themselves in the normal courts. If foreign investments are too risky, they do not happen, and this can result in the procurement base of domestic companies being insufficiently diversified.

Many countries provide guarantees for foreign investments, but only under certain conditions and if an IPT is in place, and in this case business performance indicators are particularly important. It would make sense to take the overall economic criterion of securing the supply of raw materials into account when providing guarantees. Especially in countries where the human rights situation is problematic, European investment can prompt changes for the better. But if they do not materialize, investments from countries such as China, where human rights violations play no role in the assessment of an investment location, are likely to happen. In any case, the awarding of investment guarantees should take arguments concerning geo-strategic issues and security of supply into account.

For raw materials and industrial intermediate products to reach the various regions of the world safely and at good prices a good infrastructure is required. The Chinese government pushed ahead with this many years ago: The Belt and Road Initiative is aimed precisely at opening up procurement and sales markets for China's own benefit, while development objectives take a back seat. Infrastructure such as ports and road or rail connections are in principle available to all trading partners of the countries in which they are being developed. In practice, however, it often turns out that access is not granted in equal measure and that Chinese companies are afforded an advantage. It is important that Western countries too, especially European ones, make attractive offers to countries in the Global South. Alongside the human rights situation, arguments such as security of domestic supply or geo-strategic influence should be included in investment decisions made by publicly financed development banks. In addition, the protection of transport routes must be given a higher priority. For example, Sandkamp et al.[21] provide empirical evidence that the activities of pirates on the European sea routes to and from China are having negative consequences for maritime trade.

WHAT IF DIVERSIFICATION OF SUPPLIER COUNTRIES IS IMPOSSIBLE?

It is basically impossible and inefficient to completely control all supply risks through diversification. In the case of products whose production needs major economies of scale, an increase in the number of production sites worldwide goes hand in hand with substantial cost increases. This is the case with the production of battery cells or the manufacture of computer chips. In such markets, purely market processes lead to a suboptimally small number of producers if there is a security policy externality. It is therefore reasonable to promote the foundation, establishment, or scaling of production sites in the EU (or abroad as well) using subsidies. However, it is difficult to calibrate subsidy policy correctly. The risk of subsidy races is high and there is a threat of global overcapacity.

In the case of products for which there are only a few sources of supply or where the risks associated with potential suppliers are strongly correlated, the creation of strategic warehouses may be necessary, such as in the case of oil stockpiling, which is regulated by the EU's Law on Stockpiling Petroleum and Petroleum Products. But because storage is expensive when interest rates are high, this strategy has its limits and cannot provide unconditional security of supply. The state should consider whether there should be additional tax incentives to create sufficient stocks of critical inputs. The state should ensure that companies can create storage capacity—this requires appropriate planning for land use and the approval of warehouses. And it should consider state-organized strategic storage for inputs that play a key role in many industries. The creation of a strategic gas reserve, for example along the lines of the strategic oil reserve, is a good example of this. In this case it would be important that such reserves are created and managed in an internationally coordinated manner. They should be used to manage prices, as has been done on the oil market for decades in close coordination with the US.

A second way of improving the security of supply of raw materials or intermediate products that are difficult to diversify is to promote recycling via tax and regulation. "Urban mining" is the extraction of valuable raw materials, like copper, silver and gold, from waste, such as that produced when shredding old cars—but it requires suitable facilities. In principle, it is irrelevant where this happens so long as there is multilateral access. In addition, a minimum level of planning certainty is required, because if raw material prices on the world markets fall again, the processing plants are no longer profitable. Because recycling produces significantly fewer carbon emissions than production using raw materials, high carbon pricing in the home market, combined with an effective carbon border adjustment mechanism, makes domestic processing more profitable than imports, even if world market prices fall. Finally, standards are needed for the efficient recycling of complex products, for example with regard to removing batteries easily from household appliances.

A third sensible approach is to focus research policy on researching technological substitutes for raw materials or intermediate products that are hard to diversify.

THE STATE AS A CONSUMER

In many areas, the state itself acts as a consumer, albeit often indirectly. For example, the market for medical products is dominated by demand from health insurance companies. In recent decades, efforts have been made to reduce the financial costs of the healthcare system, for example by imposing regular, compulsory discounting on the pharmaceutical industry, which has responded by outsourcing and concentrating on the cheapest suppliers. At the same time, the health insurance companies themselves do not seem to have given sufficient priority to security of supply, partly because this would have entailed additional costs. As a result, bottlenecks were created when shocks occurred. In such heavily regulated markets, the lack of diversification is not always just a result of market or management failure, but occasionally caused by government or regulatory failure.

NEW MARKETS FOR SECURITY OF SUPPLY

Finally, newly created markets can counteract the tendencies we have described towards suboptimal low diversification or stockpiling. A public sector commitment to spend money on certain products in the future is called an Advance Market Commitment (AMC). AMCs are an instrument originally proposed by Nobel prizewinner Michael Kremer at the beginning of the millennium to aid the development of drugs and vaccines to combat diseases in developing countries. The government undertakes in advance to buy a predetermined quantity of the respective product at a certain price.

If this instrument is to be used to prepare for a crisis situation, it must also be defined when exactly the public sector's commitment to buy will take effect. For example, the trigger could be that the market price of the raw material or the intermediate/final product exceeds a certain level.

If such AMCs are in place, companies can plan better for crisis situations. In particular, this reduces the worry that in these situations the government will intervene in market prices or impose taxes on (windfall) profits, since the government has previously contractually agreed to these AMCs. This makes investments in alternative supply channels and stockpiling more attractive.

Such contracts are discussed under the term "pull incentives," since the expectation of future business provides incentives for investments today—the investments are "pulled in." These are to be distinguished from "push incentives," where companies receive funds to make the respective investments, in which case the investments are "pushed."

CAPACITY MARKETS—PUSH AND PULL INCENTIVES

Often it will not be sufficient or purposeful enough to encourage companies to invest today in order to be prepared for these usually very rare crises using the expectation of guaranteed profits in times of crisis. In this case, it may also be necessary to provide financial support for this arrangement.

Capacity markets that are familiar from the electricity market and are used in the US or France, for example, do precisely this. Electricity producers apply for contracts on the capacity market in which they undertake to supply electricity at a predetermined price at certain times, for example when the electricity price exceeds a certain level. In return, they receive funds today, a payment on the capacity market.

CONFLICTING OBJECTIVES

The need to ensure that the Earth as a whole is free, just, and sustainable or at least able to contain the negative effects of shocks—climate-change-related, war-related, or technological—at a regional level encounters various kinds of difficult, conflicting objectives. On the one hand, advantages and disadvantages diverge between individuals and societies. Preventive measures that are of great benefit to the world population and large communities offer little to individual countries or even individual people, while measures that are of great benefit to a small group have little or no (positive) benefit for the world community or a country's entire population. In the literature, this problem is called the "prevention paradox."[22] To solve it requires political measures, whose conception and implementation are often made more difficult by the fact that the threats are unclear and there is a lack of experience.

In addition, in the context of the threats discussed in this essay, various distribution conflicts exist, which also always appear as conflicting objectives. In the face of impending crises, it is simply not possible to isolate some parts of the world's population from the effects of such crises without making the effects in the rest of the world even more serious. Here too, the inter-generational dimension is particularly relevant in the context of the prevention paradox, because a lack of efforts to curb climate change in the present will lead to higher adaptation costs in the future.

Even more difficult, however, is that the global cooperation necessary to curb and manage climate change is impaired by mistrust resulting from the possibility of military clashes. Robert Powell[23] showed some time ago that the ability of sovereign states to cooperate in civilian sectors (such as foreign trade) can be hugely restricted by the theoretical possibility of war. Even if no armed conflict occurs, the "shadow of war" leads to countries preemptively isolating themselves in other sectors because cooperation could create power asymmetries whose potential exploitation is a source of fear. However, it is far from clear whether reduced international cooperation, for example in trade or climate protection, would make the world more peaceful; the economic literature on this topic distinguishes between deeper multilateral cooperation, which paradoxically could make bilateral conflicts more likely because their costs would be lower due to better substitution options, and deeper bilateral cooperation, which at least reduces the likelihood of conflict between the two countries concerned.[24] Recent work confirms the empirical evidence supporting this position.

Even if economic dependencies make conflict more likely—which, as mentioned, is debatable—it is quite possible that it also makes cooperation more likely, always in each case by comparison with a situation of isolation in which neither conflict nor cooperation takes place. Against this backdrop, it seems of paramount importance that the existing international forums for cooperation are not damaged yet further, even if their usefulness is sometimes questioned even within the EU. This applies, for example, to the World Trade Organization, which sets unwelcome limits on the international safeguarding of the EU's unilateral climate protection through a border adjustment mechanism, but still offers a fundamental forum for discussing the shape of the world trade system. The same applies to the various forums of the United Nations, whose usefulness in day-to-day business is not always apparent at first glance but which, in crisis situations, can help in the exchange of essential information.

In any case, it is clear that solving the world's pressing existential problems "under the shadow of war" is particularly difficult. Ultimately, this is also because countries have to use resources to ensure their military security, resources that are sorely lacking when dealing with the climate transition or health policy challenges. In this context, peace takes priority. A free, just, and sustainable world must be a fundamentally peaceful world.

CONCLUSIONS

In order for the world to remain free, just, and sustainable for as many people as possible in as many habitats as possible, difficult distribution problems will have to be solved. If these are not resolved in an orderly manner, there is a risk of a massive escalation of political conflicts, for example through uncontrolled population displacements, resulting in new inefficiencies and shortages. To ensure that the risks that already exist do not continue to grow and, if they do occur, lead to devastating consequences—including the destruction of the Earth's habitat—investments are necessary to contain the risks and to mitigate the damage if risks materialize. This involves *ex ante* and *ex post* measures, i.e. before a crisis occurs and afterwards. Structures must be created now for both kinds of measure, but especially for the second. Some of these have been outlined in this short essay.

Since crises that can negatively affect the existence of a free, just, and sustainable world are always caused by failures in coordination, a key lesson is that the exchange of information is necessary even under adverse geopolitical circumstances and that a minimum level of cooperation is required. Because crises, when they do occur, have massive effects on distribution, clear commitments to open markets are needed in advance, because isolation undermines the market's insurance function and thus its role as an important mechanism of solidarity.

Notes

1. In addition, there are of course non-anthropogenic catastrophes such as meteorite strikes that could render the Earth uninhabitable for humankind.

2. Timothy M. Lenton, Chi Xu, Jesse F. Abrams, et al., "Quantifying the human cost of global warming" in *Nature Sustainability* 6, 2023, pp. 1237–47, https://doi.org/10.1038/s41893-023-01132-6 (accessed January 14, 2025).

3. Bojan Pancevski, "One Million Are Now Dead or Injured in the Russia-Ukraine War" in *The Wall Street Journal*, September 17, 2024, https://www.wsj.com/world/one-million-are-now-dead-or-injured-in-the-russia-ukraine-war-b09d04e5?reflink=desktopwebshare_permalink (accessed January 14, 2025).

4. William Msemburi, Ariel Karlinsky, Victoria Knutson, et al., "The WHO estimates of excess mortality associated with the COVID-19 pandemic" in *Nature* 613, 2023, pp. 130–37, https://doi.org/10.1038/s41586-022-05522-2 (accessed January 14, 2025).

5. Yuval Noah Harari, *Nexus: A Brief History of Information Networks from the Stone Age to AI* (London: Fern Press, 2024).

6. Thomas Schelling, *The Strategy of Conflict* (Cambridge, MA: Harvard University Press, 1960).

7. For a balanced presentation of the problem, see Bernhard Emunds, et al., *Raus aus der Wachstumsgesellschaft? Eine sozialethische Analyse und Bewertung von Postwachstumsstrategien*, studies by the expert panel: "Weltwirtschaft und Sozialethik", vol. 21, (Bonn: Wissenschaftliche Arbeitsgruppe für weltkirchliche Aufgaben der Deutschen Bischofskonferenz, 2018).

8. These are processes in which exponential growth takes place up to a turning point, after which the existence of a limiting factor returns the growth rate to almost zero.

9. Scott Taylor, "Innis Lecture: Environmental Crises: Past, Present, and Future" in *Canadian Journal of Economics* 15 (2), 2009, pp. 127–53.

10. James A. Brander and M. Scott Taylor, "The Simple Economics of Easter Island: A Ricardo-Malthus Model of Renewable Resource Use" in *The American Economic Review* 88 (1), 1998, pp. 119–38.

11. For an overview, see for example, Jonathan Cohen, Keith Marzilli Ericson, David Laibson, and John Myles White, "Measuring Time Preferences" in *Journal of Economic Literature* 58 (2), 2020, pp. 299–347.

12. William Nordhaus, *Managing the Global Commons: The Economics of Climate Change* (Cambridge, MA: The MIT Press, 1994).

13. Nicholas Stern, *The Economics of Climate Change: The Stern Review* (Cambridge: Cambridge University Press, 2006).

14. Benjamin Enke, Thomas Graeber, and Ryan Oprea, *Complexity and Time* (Cambridge, MA: Harvard University Press, 2024).

15. Charles Jones, "The A.I. Dilemma: Growth versus Existential Risk" in *American Economic Review: Insights* 6 (4), 2024, pp. 575–90.

16. Jones, "The A.I. Dilemma" provides a short overview of the literature.

17. Amartya Sen, *Poverty and Famines: An Essay on Entitlement and Deprivation* (Oxford: Oxford University Press 1983), https://doi.org/10.1093/0198284632.001.0001 (accessed January 14, 2025).

18. Gabriel Felbermayr and Eckhard Janeba, "Improving Supply Security: Guidelines and Policy Proposals" in *Intereconomics* 59 (3), 2024, pp. 146–53.

19. Gabriel Felbermayr and Martin Braml, *Der Freihandel hat fertig* (Vienna: Amalthea Verlag, 2024).

20. Felbermayr and Janeba, "Improving Supply Security."

21. Alexander Sandkamp, Vincent Stamer, and Shuyao Yang, "Where has the Rum Gone? The Impact of Maritime Piracy on Trade and Transport" in *Review of World Economics* 158, 2022, pp. 751–78.

22. This originates in medical literature but can be applied in lots of areas relevant to this context. It is closely related to the "commons problem" in classical economics. See Geoffrey Rose, "Strategy of Prevention: Lessons from Cardiovascular Disease" in *British Medical Journal* 282, 1981, pp. 1847–51.

23. Robert Powell, "Absolute and Relative Gains in International Relations Theory" in *The American Political Science Review* 85 (4), 1991, pp. 1303–20.

24. Philippe Martin, Thierry Mayer, and Mathias Thoenig, "Make Trade Not War?" in *The Review of Economic Studies* 75 (3), 2008, pp. 865–900.

CHAPTER 2

WHERE DOES THE POWER
TO ACT LIE?

MORITZ SCHULARICK

The question of where the power to act is located is as old as politics itself. But it has rarely been as relevant as it is today in a world that is characterized simultaneously by multiple crises and urgent systemic challenges. This essay asks where the power to act and build a free, just, and sustainable world lies today, and what role state systems of governance in particular can play in this. I will outline three fundamental dilemmas that question the ability of political systems and actors to act. The tenor of this essay is pessimistic. At a time when the demand and need for political governance is great, the capacities to govern at the most important levels are lower than they have been for a long time. The present time is characterized by the loss of these capacities, the erosion of political discourse through polarization and populism, and the increasing difficulty of global cooperation in a fragmenting world economy. Under these conditions, the scope for effective political action is limited.

THE CRISIS OF STATE CAPACITY

In Germany and other countries modern statehood is currently undergoing a serious crisis. State capacity—the ability of a state to provide public goods, regulate effectively, manage crises, and implement long-term strategies—was once a key feature of successful societies. Economic historians often emphasize that the development of administrative competence and infrastructure was one of the essential requirements that gave rise to the Industrial Revolution in the 18th and 19th centuries. In strong states such as Great Britain, France, and Prussia, a symbiosis of public and private action emerged that drove economic growth.

But today this historical model seems like a relic. The state has great difficulty managing the processes of transformation that are taking place in parallel in the areas of climate, digitalization, and demographic change. Indeed, it is even failing to manage traffic control systems, staffing in schools, and airport construction. Bureaucratic processes are outdated and inefficient, decision-making processes are lengthy, and there is a lack of courage to seek out unconventional solutions. Even projects of national importance, such as the transition to renewable energies, are stagnating.

The German state, which for a long time has been synonymous with efficiency and an ability to plan, has noticeably lost ground in international rankings. The World Bank ranks Germany fifteenth in the global ranking of state performance, and other indicators, such as the *Global Competitiveness Report*, show an even more significant decline. The decline in the quality of public infrastructure is particularly worrying— Germany dropped from third place in 2006 to twelfth in 2021.

One thing is clear: states that are able to tackle these challenges efficiently will benefit economically and ensure their political stability. The answer lies not in a "more" or "less" state, but in a "better" state, a state that operates on the basis of data, cooperates closely with science, is competent and assertive. However, this transformation is not only technological, but also cultural—it requires a break with old structures and patterns of thinking that have proven to be a hindrance. In this respect we are at best just at the beginning. Pessimistically, we might say that we are moving, but so slowly that the gap between Germany and other countries is continuing to grow.

POLARIZATION AND POPULISM: THE EROSION OF PUBLIC DISCOURSE

At the same time, we can see how the conditions for successful political decision-making are eroding. Populism and polarization have created a vicious circle of mistrust, simplification, and deadlock in many democracies. Populists portray society as a dualistic system—"the people" versus "the elites"—and offer simple solutions to complex problems. This kind of rhetoric is particularly successful in times of crisis, whether during the 2008 financial crisis, the 2015 refugee crisis, or the COVID-19 pandemic.

We live in an age of populism. Never before have populists been in power in so many countries. The year 2018 held the previous record with sixteen countries governed by populists, including Brazil, Bulgaria, Greece, Mexico, Poland, the Philippines, Slovakia,

Hungary, and the US. Measured by economic output, these countries account for more than 30 percent of global gross domestic product.

The impact is disastrous: societies shaped by populism lose the ability to engage in critical public discourse, to compromise, and to make long-term, reliable plans. Political debates degenerate into mudslinging in which facts and rational arguments are afforded less and less space. Polarization extends to all areas of social life, from the media landscape to science, and prevents consensus building and the development of a critical public sphere, which would be needed to be able to take courageous political action in times of transformation.

Populist rhetoric feeds on a sense of powerlessness and dissatisfaction that is often exacerbated by economic or social crises. But instead of offering solutions, it makes the problems worse: polarization inhibits political decision-making and endangers democratic stability. The data is clear: countries governed by populists often experience increased levels of social inequality, slower economic growth, and an erosion of democratic institutions and freedom of the press.

FRAGILE HOPE FOR GLOBAL COOPERATION

The third problem is the decreasing ability to cooperate globally. Globalization, for a long time the engine of economic development, has not led to a safer or more stable world despite its economic successes in recent decades. Today it is faltering, and we may even be entering a phase of deglobalization.

Historically, the production of global public goods—such as climate protection, trade security, or pandemic prevention—was often coordinated by a hegemon. The US has occupied this role for decades, but today the US itself is weakened by political instability and its own slide into nationalism and populism, and is no longer able to play this role. At the same time, China and India are advancing into the global arena with their own agendas. Both countries have their own interests and worldviews that often clash with those of the West and the Atlantic alliance. Geopolitical rivalries and the formation of new blocs are dominating the scene. In a time of growing geopolitical tensions, global cooperation seems increasingly unrealistic. The quasi-hegemonic era in which the US foreign policy of multilateralism guaranteed a framework of global cooperation is over. The world is shifting from a win-win logic to a zero-sum game logic in which the gains of one's opponent are perceived as one's own losses.

From a German perspective, crisis-ridden Europe remains the only credible alternative to help shape a free, just, and sustainable world at a global level. Europe offers hope, albeit a fragile one. The EU Single Market shows how economic integration and political cooperation can go hand in hand. But the EU is also facing the challenge of proving its ability to act in the increasingly self-sufficient world of the G3—US, China, and the EU. Europe's system of governance is under pressure. Internal tensions and external threats from authoritarian regimes pose major challenges to the "European peace project." As Europe's major economy, Germany must decide whether it wants to actively shape the vision of a strong and capable Europe as a global political actor or accept that Europe will become a plaything tossed between the US and China. One thing is clear: If we as Europeans want to continue shaping the course of the world, we must also be willing to take risks, including financial ones, instead of retreating into our German shell as mere onlookers.

CONCLUSION

The conclusion of this essay is sobering. In our era of rapid and multidimensional transformations, the need for state governance over ecological and technological processes in order to shape a free, just, and sustainable world has rarely been as urgent as it is today. Climate change and the transition to renewable energy sources require coordinated measures and complex economic policies on an unprecedented scale. At the same time, aging populations are putting pressure on social systems and require a restructuring of public spending. At the international level, the disintegration of the globalization project, rising protectionism, and new geopolitical rivalries pose significant risks to the possibility of international cooperation.

The instrument needed to manage these transformations—the state—seems increasingly unable to act and appears to have only a limited ability to perform these tasks. Polarization and populism are paralyzing political discourse. If the state fails to meet these challenges, the overlapping crises of our age are likely to deepen. The way forward requires a rebuilding of the state's capacities to govern. This includes investments in education, effective governance, and global cooperation. But implementing these goals in polarized political environments and in the face of global uncertainty is a Herculean task.

Perhaps a glimmer of hope exists in the shape of technological innovation. Radical breakthroughs in the areas of energy, digitalization, and mobility could reduce the economic and social costs of the current transformations and thus reduce the scale of the problem of governance, so that we can get through the next decade with stability, even in a time of limited capacities to govern. This path too is of course full of risks. New technologies also always mean new political challenges and concentrate political and economic power in the hands of a few. But this too is something for which the political system is still poorly prepared.

CHAPTER 3

HOW CAN WE CREATE A FREE, JUST, AND SUSTAINABLE WORLD? THE ROLE OF GLOBAL GOVERNANCE

PHILIPP PATTBERG

INTRODUCTION

To achieve a truly free, just, and sustainable future, we need deep transformations in terms of our technological, economic, and political systems, as well as underlying norms and values. While this challenge is acknowledged and discussed in relation to the domestic context—the state and its citizens—an important element has been neglected: the role of the international system and global governance in achieving a free, just, and sustainable world.

Two distinct questions emerge: First, how does a failure to achieve a free, just, and sustainable world affect the international system? In other words, can the current international architecture of cooperation and rules-based multilateralism be sustained under conditions of rapid social and environmental destabilization? And second, what reforms of the multilateral system are needed to support the sustainability transformation at all levels? In other words, how can we make multilateralism work better for a free, just, and sustainable future? I will deal with the latter question in this short contribution, as the former is treated elsewhere.[1]

This contribution is structured in three parts. First, I review the symptoms and causes of the polycrisis and its relation to the international system. Second, I briefly describe the current institutions of global governance before, third, I elaborate on reform options for ensuring a free, just, and sustainable future.

THE POLYCRISIS AND THE INTERNATIONAL
SYSTEM

Building on the 1993 book *Terre-Patrie*, published in English as *Homeland Earth*,[2] the term polycrisis describes a complex situation where multiple, interconnected crises overlap and amplify each other, resulting in a situation that is difficult to manage or resolve. For example, food systems are under stress due to a number of seemingly isolated but interconnected issues, including environmental threats, international conflicts, and pandemics. Other elements of polycrisis include the climate crisis, the crisis of underdevelopment and inequality, growing economic imbalance induced by technology-driven growth, AI, the rise of social media and information wars, populism, and the global health crisis, to name just a few.

The concept of polycrisis also builds on insights from the academic field of complexity studies, highlighting the fact that complex systems produce emerging properties which can not be reduced to the sum of their individual parts.[3] The situation of a polycrisis can therefore be understood as a wicked problem—one that is difficult or even impossible to solve due to incomplete information and changing requirements that are hard to recognize. Therefore, the concept of polycrisis might equip us to see beyond single problems and recognize potentially unintended side effects that interventions may have on other crucial systems.[4]

The international system, understood here as the international state system and its transnational extensions,[5] provides the context in which, politically speaking, the polycrisis and its constituent parts must be addressed. However, the international system, or more precisely current world order, is in crisis as well. Referred to variously as the contestation of the global rules-based order, the end of the liberal democratic "West," the new multi-polar, reality or a "Cold War" 2.0, the international system is moving out of its hegemonic and unipolar moment into a more complex and murkier situation. This new "bricolage" has three important characteristics.

Let us first briefly consider the rise of authoritarianism, referring to the increasing prevalence of centralized, non-democratic governance where power is concentrated in the hands of a single leader or a small elite. Authoritarian regimes are characterized by absence of political pluralism, diminished civil liberties, restricted freedom of expression and the press, and more generally speaking the suppression of dissent.

Several factors have contributed to the global resurgence of authoritarianism in recent years, including economic, technological, and political factors. Economic instability and inequality often create fertile ground for authoritarian tendencies as citizens, frustrated with ineffective democratic governance and unfair distribution of wealth, may seek strong, decisive leadership. Populist leaders frequently exploit these grievances, promoting populist nationalism and undermining democratic norms under the guise of restoring order and national strength. In addition, technological advancements have also played a significant role in facilitating authoritarianism. Consider for example digital surveillance, control over online discourses, and the spread of disinformation all of which allow authoritarian regimes to manufacture consent while suppressing opposition. Social media, while under certain conditions a tool for positive change, has also become a platform for authoritarian propaganda and manipulation.[6] International factors, such as the decline of Western hegemony and the rise of powers like China and Russia, have further emboldened authoritarian regimes. These states often promote alternative governance models emphasizing stability and economic growth over democratic freedoms (see also the third point below).

Consequently, the rise of authoritarianism not only leads to human rights abuses, suppression of free expression, and the marginalization of minority groups, but authoritarian regimes can also destabilize the international order, as they often reject cooperative global norms in favor of unilateral actions and more aggressive foreign policy.

A second characteristic of the international system in crisis is the return of protectionism, referring to the resurgence of policies aimed at shielding domestic industries from foreign competition through tariffs, quotas, and regulatory barriers. This shift marks a departure from the post-World War II trend toward trade liberalization, which was institutionalized through the GATT and later the WTO, strengthening Western, neo-liberal hegemony in the international system. The key drivers of resurgent protectionism include economic nationalism, rising inequality, and geopolitical tensions. Governments, particularly in developed economies, have increasingly adopted protectionist measures in response to deindustrialization and job losses attributed to stiff global competition and outsourcing. The 2008 global financial crisis further fueled skepticism toward globalization, as protectionist rhetoric gained traction amid stagnant wages and economic insecurity.[7] Further compounded by technological change and supply chain vulnerabilities, especially exposed during the COVID-19 pandemic, this has led to increased calls for securing critical industries.

Let us consider a third characteristic of world order in crisis: emerging alliances against the West. At a time when the G7 is trying to retain the power to define global rules, Russia and China are working in tandem to destabilize this narrative and establish intuitional alternatives, for example in the form of the BRICS+ initiative. In the words of one critical observer:

> BRICS expansion evidences a growing global dissatisfaction with and a determination to challenge the structural advantages that advanced market democracies continue to enjoy in a global order that was in many respects made by the West, for the West. Reducing those exorbitant privileges, including by creating alternative, parallel institutions, is the fundamental purpose of BRICS+.[8]

Taken together, the normative idea of a rules-based international system evolving around the United Nations and core values of sovereignty, self-determination, peaceful relations, and sustainability, are severely under pressure. How can key features of the contemporary world order be sustained while important parts are renewed to ensure a free, fair, and sustainable future? The next sections will consider the current form of global governance, its shortcomings, and subsequent reform needs.

GLOBAL GOVERNANCE

World affairs are currently governed by a loosely coupled system of international and transnational institutions, collectively referred to as global governance. International and transnational institutions are pivotal components of global governance, structuring the way states, non-state actors, and international organizations coordinate and manage global affairs. Though both categories play critical roles in facilitating cooperation and addressing cross-border challenges, they differ in scope, authority, and operational mechanisms.

International institutions refer to formal, treaty-based organizations established by sovereign states to promote cooperation on specific issues of mutual interest and to international law in a broader sense, including treaties, conventions, and protocols. Some international institutions possess legal personality, meaning they can enter into agreements and possess rights and obligations under international law. Their primary functions include setting norms, facilitating negotiations, monitoring compliance, and sometimes enforcing decisions. Key examples include the United Nations (UN) and its specialized agencies and programs, the World Trade Organization (WTO), and the International Monetary Fund (IMF). These institutions are primarily state-centric, with membership limited to recognized sovereign states. Decision-making structures vary but often reflect principles of state sovereignty and equality (one country, one vote), although power imbalances can influence institutional dynamics, for instance in case of the UN Security Council that grants veto powers only to its five permanent members. In addition to formal international organizations, global governance is also pursued through international agreements on specific problems, such as the Paris Agreement on climate change, the Convention on Biological Diversity on biodiversity, and the Montreal Protocol on the phase-out of ozone-depleting substances, to name just a few of an estimated 1,000 international environmental/sustainability-related treaties.[9]

In addition to the more formal international system, there is also a densely populated system of transnational institutions that involve a broader range of actors, including multinational corporations (MNCs), non-governmental organizations (NGOs), advocacy networks, and epistemic communities. These actors often operate across national boundaries without direct state control, emphasizing global cooperation through non-state mechanisms. Examples include the International Chamber of Commerce (ICC), Médecins Sans Frontières (Doctors Without Borders), and advocacy groups like Amnesty International. Unlike international institutions, transnational entities may not derive their authority from treaties but instead gain influence through market forces, public opinion, moral authority, and the ability to solve problems "on the ground."

Transnational actors play a crucial role in norm-setting, capacity-building, and policy advocacy. For instance, Transparency International influences global anti-corruption norms, while MNCs such as Google and Apple shape digital governance practices. Additionally, transnational advocacy networks often pressure governments and international organizations to adopt more progressive policies, as seen in global climate activism. Next to non-state actors who operate in the transnational sphere, there also exist transnational rule-systems and regulations, comparable to the host of international treaties and agreements. For example, the non-state Forest Stewardship

Council (and many other global certification schemes) sets globally applicable rules for the sustainable and fair production and distribution of timber without the involvement of governments.

While distinct, international and transnational institutions frequently intersect and collaborate. Global climate governance exemplifies this interplay: The UN Framework Convention on Climate Change (UNFCCC) operates as an international institution providing a formal negotiation platform, while transnational groups like the Climate Action Network (CAN) influence public opinion and policy proposals within the UNFCCC framework. Moreover, transnational institutions often fill gaps left by international institutions, particularly in areas where state cooperation is limited or politically sensitive. For example, NGOs provide humanitarian aid in conflict zones where state actors cannot operate due to sovereignty constraints. It is important to note that, while distinct but intersecting, transnational and international institutions, as key components of global governance, are underwritten by a few core values, such as liberalism, the primacy of markets, and individual (rather than collective) freedoms.

REFORM OPTIONS FOR ACHIEVING FREEDOM, FAIRNESS, AND SUSTAINABILITY

Against the background of current global governance practices and the ongoing challenge to a rules-based world order, what reform options exist that could have the potential to secure a free, fair, and sustainable future for all?

Before outlining such reform options, let me briefly reiterate the obstacles. A first set of obstacles derives from shortcomings in the current global governance system, including consensus-based decision-making at the UN level, vested interests and power structures that guard against transformative change, a focus on issues and sectoral problems instead of a more holistic approach taking into account the complex and interdependent nature of the polycrisis, and a set of values oriented at economic growth and individual entitlements. And as a more generalized observation, current global institutions are not equipped to deal with massive social disruptions on a global scale, for example disruptions related to climate change.[10]

A second set of obstacles derives from the fact that the current (imperfect) global order is increasingly challenged, resulting in a weakening of norms and rules. The rise of authoritarian tendencies, both in democratic and non-democratic societies, the reorientation towards economic protectionism, and the strengthening of anti-Western, anti-liberal international alliances works against both the existing global governance system and its problem-solving abilities as well as against possible reform.

I will now turn to five options for reform of our global governance system that could enable a transition to a truly free, just, and sustainable future for all.

The first element of reform is increasing inclusiveness of decision-making at the global level. Current global decision-making structures often reflect historical power imbalances, with disproportionate influence wielded by a few powerful states, as seen in the UN Security Council and international financial institutions like the IMF and World Bank. This limited inclusiveness has led to perceptions of global governance as unrepresentative and biased towards the interests of wealthier nations. Consequently, a reform aimed at increasing inclusiveness involves expanding representation and participation of underrepresented states, especially those from the Global South, in key decision-making bodies. This could involve restructuring voting systems to reflect contemporary economic and demographic realities, ensuring broader regional representation, and giving emerging economies a greater voice in global institutions. Moreover, inclusiveness extends beyond state actors. Non-state entities, such as civil society organizations, indigenous groups, and marginalized communities, should be better integrated into global policy discussions. Mechanisms like consultative forums, stakeholder panels, citizen assemblies, and public consultations are gaining traction and could enhance participation, ensuring diverse perspectives to influence policy outcomes.

The second element is future orientation in decision-making. Including future generations in decision-making is essential for ensuring long-term sustainability, justice, and accountability in global governance as many policy choices made today—on climate change, resource extraction, debt accumulation, and technological development—will have profound consequences for those yet to be born. However, current decision-making processes often prioritize short-term interests, neglecting the well-being of future populations. By institutionalizing mechanisms such as ombudspersons for future generations, intergenerational impact assessments, and future-oriented sustainability councils, governance structures can better incorporate the rights and interests of those not yet represented. This approach aligns with principles of intergenerational equity, ensuring that the benefits and burdens of policy decisions are fairly distributed over time. Including future generations also encourages a more precautionary, forward-looking mindset in policy design, fostering resilience and sustainability in global systems. One important milestone on the way to better integrating future generations into current decision-making is the adoption of the Declaration on Future Generations as part of the 2024 Summit of the Future outcome documents.[11]

Like proposals to better represent future generations, there is a need to better safeguard the interests of non-human entities, including abstract nature such as rivers, mountains, and landscapes. This larger debate can be subsumed under the idea of "rights for nature," arguing for improved legal representation of nature, or simply put, the recognition that nature has rights. While the concept is contested in political debate, we see increased lobbying for its acceptance (for example the recently established Global Alliance for the Rights of Nature), signifying a pivotal point in our representation of nature in global governance debates.

Another important element of a global governance system fit for purpose is its ability to deal with massive societal disruptions. While the precise mechanisms for dealing with the implications of the polycrisis will vary depending on what aspect of its interconnected features will be addressed, it is fair to say that appropriate mechanisms will have to address burden-sharing, adaptation, compensation, and supporting creative ways of dealing with breakdown (on a collective level).

Finally, urgent reforms of the current global governance system are needed to overcome the predominant silo approach and to genuinely deliver on the promise of nexus governance. More information-sharing, collaboration, and joint decision-making among various international organizations and treaties, for example the climate change and biodiversity regimes, is slowly emerging. However, this is an ad hoc process and not yet sufficiently embedded in the overall global governance system.

To summarize, in this essay I have argued that effective global governance, i.e. international and transnational institutions, is needed to build a free, just, and sustainable world of tomorrow out of the polycrisis of today. However, global governance is both working suboptimally and, at the same time, being challenged by powerful actors and interests. The rules-based international order, a cornerstone of global governance, is being challenged from both inside and outside: from the inside by short-sighted populistic, nationalistic, and protectionist tendencies, and from the outside by actors who challenge the status quo in a moment of weakness and lack of leadership.

To make global governance fit for purpose, I have suggested five areas of reform: inclusive decision-making, future-orientation, rights for nature, adapting to breakdown, and realizing the nexus approach. Each of these reform agendas is hard to realize in the context of the polycrisis. But by working on them step by step, we are building, piece by piece, the foundations of a free, just, and sustainable future for all.

Notes

1. Philipp Pattberg, *Rethinking Climate Governance* (Cheltenham: Edward Elgar, forthcoming).

2. Edgar Morin and Anne-Brigitte Kern, *Homeland Earth* (New York: Hampton Press, 1999).

3. Philipp Pattberg in Klaus F. Zimmermann (ed.), *Handbook of Labor, Human Resources and Population Economics* (Cham, Switzerland: Springer Nature, 2025).

4. For example, Mike Hulme, *Climate Change Isn't Everything: Liberating Climate Politics from Alarmism* (Cambridge: Polity Press, 2023).

5. Ryūhei Hatsuse, "International System, Government and Politics" in Vol. II, *UNESCO – Encyclopedia of Life Support Systems* (EOLSS), 2023.

6. Paolo Gerbaudo, "Social Media and Populism: An Elective Affinity?" in *Media, Culture & Society*, 40 (5), 2018, pp. 745–53, https://doi.org/10.1177/0163443718772192 (accessed January 7, 2025).

7. Simon J. Evenett, "Protectionism, State Discrimination, and International Business since the Onset of the Global Financial Crisis" in *Journal of International Business Policy* 2, 2019, pp. 9–36, https://doi.org/10.1057/s42214-019-00021-0 (accessed January 7, 2025).

8. Stewart Patrick, "BRICS Expansion, the G20, and the Future of World Order" (Carnegie Endowment for International Peace, 2024), https://carnegieendowment.org/research/2024/10/brics-summit-emerging-middle-powers-g7-g20?lang=en (accessed January 3, 2025).

9. Ronald B. Mitchell, Liliana B. Andonova, Mark Axelrod, Jörg Balsiger, Thomas Bernauer, Jessica F. Green, James Hollway, Rakhyun E. Kim, and Jean-Frédéric Morin, "What We Know (and Could Know) about International Environmental Agreements" in *Global Environmental Politics* 20 (1), 2020, pp. 103–21, https://doi.org/10.1162/glep_a_00544 (accessed January 7, 2025).

10. See Jem Bendell, Breaking Together: A Freedom-loving Response to Collapse (Bristol: Good Works, 2023); Frank Biermann, "The Future of 'Environmental' Policy in the Anthropocene: Time for a Paradigm shift" in *Environmental Politics*, 30 (1–2), 2020, pp. 61–80, https://www.tandfonline.com/doi/full/10.1080/09644016.2020.1846958 (accessed January 7, 2025).

11. United Nations, Pact for the Future, Global Digital Compact and Declaration on Future Generations, 2024, https://www.un.org/sites/un2.un.org/files/sotf-pact_for_the_future_adopted.pdf, (accessed January 7, 2025).

CHAPTER 4

THE CHALLENGE OF CLIMATE CHANGE—WHAT CAN THE LAW ACHIEVE?

CHRISTINE LANGENFELD

I. CONSTITUTIONAL DEMOCRACY AND CLIMATE PROTECTION

Today, the rule of law and democracy are under pressure worldwide, even in Germany. It is feared that the institutions of constitutional democracy are being undermined. What does this mean when it comes to dealing with challenges such as climate change?[1] How can intergenerational climate justice be achieved in a democratic society? First of all, democracy and the rule of law are not up for discussion. Dismantling democracy and the rule of law in order to implement the necessary climate protection is out of the question. Therefore, climate protection requires democratic majorities. Achieving these is anything but easy, even if the challenge of climate change is acknowledged in principle by most of the population. But when things get real, when cuts, changes, and unreasonable demands are made in the course of the necessary transformation, things look different. A future-oriented climate protection policy that also takes account of future generations conflicts with the lack of willingness to change on the part of considerable sections of the population and the related short-termism of politicians who are thinking about election cycles and their re-election. On the other hand, given the existential challenge of climate change and the associated task of transformation, a broad social consensus is needed to constructively support and democratically legitimize this transformation process. Any blockages must be overcome by a convincing discourse that creates trust, because the idea that we can carry on as before, that everything can stay as it was, means turning a blind eye to reality and is therefore irrational and destructive but nonetheless widespread, because this is exactly what (right-wing) populist parties are promising. Climate protection policy is being discredited as a project of the elites. So far politicians have only managed to counter this to a limited extent using a convincing narrative that presents sustainability as the goal of a transformation, precisely in order to maintain a good life and prosperity both in the future and over the long term. This narrative stimulates the willingness of the majority to tackle the necessary changes in order to achieve this goal, even if these changes are initially associated with unreasonable demands.

These considerations lead us to conclude that strengthening constitutional democracies to resist the temptations of populism—in Germany, but also elsewhere—is a prerequisite for successfully tackling climate change. Whether this succeeds depends crucially on people's trust in the ability of the democratic constitutional state to deal with the challenge of climate change. Despite all the controversies that exist, particularly those on how to deal with climate change in democratic states, there is much to suggest that constitutional democracies are best suited to facing up to the reality of climate change and taking measures to contain and adapt to it. This is because democracies are capable of self-reflection and self-correction.

In functioning democracies, the fact of climate change cannot be denied given a free media and a free culture of debate. On the other hand, restrictions and changes undertaken against the will of the population cannot simply be imposed in a democracy. The political elites must react to this and face up to the citizens' electoral decisions. A climate dictatorship is not an alternative and is excluded under a liberal constitution.

In light of all of this, it is clear that climate change cannot be addressed without solid constitutional and democratic institutions, at least not in a way that focuses on the individual, their freedom, but also their responsibilities. Climate change must be tackled in a way that is both constitutional and socially accept- able. In the interests of its long-term acceptance by citizens and businesses, the necessary change must be approached with a sense of proportion, openness to innovation, and flexibility. The changes required to deal with climate change, which often involve restrictions on freedom or a change in fundamental conditions, must be shaped in accordance with consti- tutional principles. To this extent, the presumption of the fundamental freedom of the individual applies; infringements of this freedom must be justified and must be based on the principles of proportionality, the welfare state, protection of legitimate expectations, and legal certainty.

II. THE ROLE OF THE COURTS—WHAT DO "CLIMATE LAWSUITS" ACHIEVE?

Laws that serve to combat climate change or adapt to climate change must be created by democratically legitimized legislators. These laws are then implemented and enforced by the authorities and the courts. This climate protection is happening every day through the implementation of the relevant specialized legislation. One aspect of this implementation are the so-called "climate lawsuits," which can be divided into three categories.[2]

The first category includes lawsuits by individuals or environmental protection organizations against private companies. In Germany, a lawsuit filed by a Peruvian farmer against RWE, Germany's largest electricity company, has generated a lot of attention. The farmer is demanding that the company pay some of the costs of protecting his house, measures he claims are necessary because carbon emissions produced by RWE have caused a glacier to melt, and the melt-water flowing into a nearby lake has raised the water level, thus threatening the farmer's house and village. The lawsuit was dismissed at first instance.[3] It is now pending an appeal before the Higher Regional Court of Hamm, which took an on-site hearing of evidence in May 2022.[4] The decision is still pending.[5] In The Hague, Netherlands, a court of first instance admitted a lawsuit against Shell to reduce corporate greenhouse gas emissions by 45 percent by 2030.[6] The company was forced to cut its oil production by almost one half, while its competitors are allowed to continue producing without restrictions. Following Shell's appeal, the first instance judgment was overturned.[7] Shell has now moved its headquarters from the Netherlands to London. Such private lawsuits enjoy considerable public profile, but ultimately they do nothing to combat climate change. Their problems are obvious: they are to do with causality and also the fact that companies are thereby held liable for actions that were lawful. These actions were and are part of a highly complex system of resource extraction and use that forms the basis of the today's economic model. It is highly questionable whether private companies that create the conditions for this, as representatives of this model so to speak, can and should be held liable for doing so.

The second category of climate lawsuits includes those brought before the administrative courts, a large number of which are also pending in Germany. The plaintiffs are often supported by environmental organizations who are adopting a strategic approach in doing so. Such lawsuits invoke the inadequate application of the relevant specialized law on climate protection. Some of them are quite successful, as they are about the implementation of specific legislative standards.

This is to be distinguished from the third category of climate lawsuits, which we will discuss in conclusion. These are lawsuits against measures or omissions by the legislature that are brought before constitutional and supreme courts. It was in response to such a lawsuit, or more precisely a constitutional complaint, that the famous climate decision of the First Senate of Germany's Federal Constitutional Court was issued in March 2021.[8] With this decision, the Court declared the then Federal Climate Action Act[9] to be incompatible with the Basic Law. Specialized courts are not authorized to make such a ruling. If constitutional courts establish constitutional standards for climate protection, democratically passed laws can be repealed if a constitutional court has the appropriate authority. Often, as in the case of this climate decision, the reasons for this incompatibility as given by the court result in further standards for the legislature, for example in the form of orders and reduction targets that the legislature must implement, as was the case in the climate decision mentioned above.

Thus, a structural tension exists between constitutional courts on the one hand, and the democratic principle and the separation of powers on the other hand. This tension is inherent in a strong constitutional jurisdiction. Constitutional courts must be conscious of this situation, because this tension can have an impact on the acceptability of their decisions and on the willingness of states and citizens to comply with them. The Federal Constitutional Court's climate protection decision takes this into account and—contrary to what is often claimed—gives the legislature considerable leeway in implementing the climate targets set out in the constitution. These targets are based on the carbon budget to which Germany is entitled according to the Paris Agreement,[10] and to which Germany has also agreed. Exceeding this budget would drive global warming beyond the Paris targets. These targets, on which the German legislature has also based its climate protection legislation in fulfilment of the climate protection requirement in the Basic Law, are also decisive for the Constitutional

Court's review, subject to new scientific findings on the effects of global warming or how carbon emissions are dealt with, which legislators must take into account. The argument ("drop in the ocean" objection) that Germany's efforts cannot make a decisive contribution to combating climate change on a global scale does not change this obligation, since, according to the Paris Agreement, every state is obliged to achieve the goals set out therein within the scope of its responsibilities. The Paris goals of keeping global warming at 1.5 degrees if possible and significantly below 2 degrees are therefore part of the constitutional requirements for climate protection (Article 20a of the Basic Law). Freedom rights now require that legislators take the interests of future generations into account when implementing this obligation. It is about protecting intergenerational freedoms, which states that legislators must ensure that the carbon budget available until climate neutrality is achieved in 2050 is distributed in such a way that no massive restrictions on freedom occur at a later date (in this case from 2031) because there is very little or no carbon left available. Nevertheless, in order to comply with the Paris targets, numerous activities protected by fundamental rights—and which are relevant to carbon—must then be highly restricted. A law that allows the rapid consumption of our budget over the coming years, as the first climate protection law did until 2030, thus has an advance interference-like effect on freedom rights from 2031 onwards. The Federal Constitutional Court considered this to be disproportionate, because it is unreasonable that people today are allowed to emit more pollutants than those who will be alive in eight or ten years, given that more far-reaching and acceptable options for making savings are available today. This means that the court is required to achieve a proportionate balance between current and future freedoms. How legislators achieve this apportionment and what measures they take to achieve this—this could include, for example, the expansion of carbon pricing—is up to the legislature, and also depends on developments in technology and science. Ultimately, only obvious and gross failures to comply with proportionality can cause the legislative measures taken to become unconstitutional. The ball is therefore in the court of democratically legitimized legislators, but the goal is set by the constitution and is therefore binding for the legislature. Monitoring compliance with existing constitutional requirements in the area of climate protection is what constitutional and supreme courts can and should do. With all due caution, it can be said that this understanding of the role of constitutional and supreme courts in the area of climate protection seems to be developing in the multilevel cooperation taking place between Europe's constitutional courts, at least insofar as the courts have related competences and viable points of reference in their constitutions. The beginnings of this could already be seen at a conference organized by the Federal Constitutional Court in Berlin in 2023 on the topic of "Climate protection challenges facing constitutional and supreme courts."[11]

Climate lawsuits are also playing an increasing role at international level. At EU level, ten families from the EU, Kenya, and Fiji sued the European Parliament and the Council in the so-called "People's Climate Case." They wanted to see a tightening of the EU's climate targets. The lawsuit was declared inadmissible by the Court of First Instance (CFI) and the European Court of Justice (ECJ), as the plaintiffs were not individually affected.[12] By contrast, a complaint brought before the European Court of Human Rights (ECtHR) by Swiss senior citizens and the group they founded, invoking the right to respect for one's private and family life (Art. 8) and the right to life (Art. 2) in the Convention, was successful. The Court upheld the complaint—quite surprisingly in the opinion of experts.[13] It derived detailed requirements for national climate protection measures from the right to private and family life and thus confirmed that Switzerland had violated the Convention.[14] Furthermore, the Court concluded, Switzerland had not granted the group of "KlimaSeniorinnen" sufficient access to a court, so that there was also a violation of the Convention's guarantee of legal protection (Art. 6). In this matter, the Court draws on the climate protection agreements signed by the contracting states, namely the 1992 United Nations Framework Convention on Climate Change[15] and the Paris Climate Agreement of 2015, to outline the states' duties of protection within the framework of the Convention's guarantees. Fulfilling the states' promise to contribute to reducing emissions within this framework can thus be made legally binding. At the same time, the ECtHR—like the Federal Constitutional Court in its climate protection decision—emphasizes the responsibility of legislators. Climate protection measures, according to the ECtHR, are to a large extent the job of democratically legitimized legislators. The task of the courts therefore complements the democratic process. The judiciary ensures the monitoring of compliance with the legal obligations entered into by states.

It cannot be denied that the ECtHR ruling has met with intense criticism in Switzerland.[16] The Swiss People's Party described the decision as "brazen interference by foreign judges in Swiss politics" and even called for Switzerland's withdrawal from the Council of Europe. Public criticism culminated in a vote by Switzerland's Federal Assembly not to comply with the ECtHR ruling. The Council of States and then the National Council too accused the Strasbourg judges of judicial activism, and claimed that the Court had invented a new human right to climate protection that was not mentioned in the Convention. Now the Swiss Federal Council has also looked at the Strasbourg ruling. In its statement, it first reaffirms Switzerland's commitment to membership of the Council of Europe and the ECtHR, then states that Switzerland has already fulfilled the requirements of the ruling through the revised CO_2 Act of March 15, 2024.[17] This is not the place to critique Switzerland's position in detail. However, the Swiss reaction makes it clear that dealing with climate change raises key questions about the separation of powers and the role of the judiciary, especially the international judiciary, in their assessment of the relevant human rights.

III. THE STRUCTURAL LIMITS AND EFFICACY OF SUPREME COURT JUDGMENTS ON CLIMATE ISSUES

1.) What are supreme courts unable to achieve structurally in the area of climate protection, by contrast? Beyond judicial restraint and the separation of powers, the implementation of climate protection measures—in the form of both emissions reduction and adaptation measures—requires highly complex decisions concerning balance and prioritization that affect an entire society, an entire economy, and in particular the highly developed economies. They address changes that demand lots of individual steps and measures. Courts are already structurally unable to do this. The shape of this transformation process must be negotiated and decided democratically. Constitutional courts, however, do not shape; they exercise powers of veto. They can declare laws to be unconstitutional. They can consider the actions of legislators to be inadequate in terms of the constitution's requirements for climate protection and they can force the legislature to deal with the challenge of climate change. In this way, they can support legislators when they adopt climate protection measures that place demands upon citizens and change hitherto familiar patterns. Courts can help legislators to break through the kind of short-termism in political decision-making that typically prevails in a democracy. They can oblige them to create incentives to implement emission-reducing activities. But this is no substitute for democratically legitimized and shaping climate protection policies.

2.) National climate protection decisions only apply to the respective state. The question arises whether this really makes sense in view of the indisputable fact that climate protection can only be achieved through international cooperation and that measures taken by individual nations in the form of bans, emission reductions, etc. may just weaken the country's own economy without contributing anything relevant to climate protection. First of all, it would be disastrous for climate protection if every state were to say to itself: I can't do anything anyway on my own. If we adopted this way of thinking, no one would do anything. Equally, in light of the cumulative effects of carbon emissions, every state is called upon to reduce its emissions in fulfilment of the international obligations it has entered into, even if its own share of harmful emissions is very small. It is also consistent with this situation that the Basic Law's climate protection requirement also obliges the state to seek a solution to the climate protection problem by cooperating at an international level. According to its climate protection decision, Germany is leading the way in this and is a role model in the hope and expectation that other states will follow this example and enable effective climate protection. In order for this to happen, and because the German example is attractive to other states, we need a convincing and effective climate protection policy that takes into account economic and social circumstances and is open to technological developments and innovations. Designing and shaping such a policy will probably be the decisive challenge in the coming years and decades.

Notes

1. For a helpful discussion of the below, see Ulrich Maidowski, "Intertemporale Klimagerechtigkeit in der demokratischen Gesellschaft" in *perspektive mediation* 2, 2024, p. 119, https://biblioscout.net/journal/pm (accessed January 31, 2025).

2. Cf. also the overview with examples of the categories of lawsuit described below given in Wolfgang Kahl, Klaus Ferdinand, and Jacqueline Lorenzen, § 6 VII. "Climate Change Litigation," pp. 251 ff., in Wolfgang Kahl and Klaus Ferdinand Gärditz, *Umweltrecht*, 13th edn. (Munich: C.H. Beck, 2023).

3. Essen Regional Court, Judgment of December 15, 2016 - 2 O 285/15 -, NVwZ 2017, 734.

4. Hamm Higher Regional Court, press release of June 17, 2022,

Evidence taking in Peru in the case of Luciano Lliuya v. RWE AG, https://www.olg-hamm.nrw.de/behoerde/presse/Pressemitteilungen/zt-Archiv/2022_Pressearchiv/19_22_PE_Beweisaufnahme-in-Peru-im-Rechtsstreit-Lliuya-___-RWE/index.php (accessed February 10, 2025).

5. According to Germanwatch, the organization that is supporting the plaintiff, a date for a court hearing is still to be set, https://rwe.climatecase.org/en (accessed January 31, 2025).

6. The Hague District Court, May 26, 2021, C/09/571932/HA ZA 19-379 https://uitspraken.rechtspraak.nl/inziendocument?id=ECLI:NL:RBDHA:2021:5339 (accessed January 31, 2025).

7. The Hague Court of Appeal, November 12, 2024, 200.302.332/01 https://uitspraken.rechtspraak.nl/details?id=ECLI:NL:GHDHA:2024:2100 (accessed January 31, 2025). An appeal to the Dutch Supreme Court remains available.

8. Federal Constitutional Court, Order of March 24, 2021 - 1 BvR 2656/18, 78/20, 96/20, 288/20 -, NVwZ 2021, 1723.

9. Federal Climate Action Act of December 12, 2019 (BGBl 2019 I S. 2513).

10. Paris Agreement of December 12, 2015, United Nations, Treaty Series, vol. 3156, p. 79, came into force on November 4, 2016.

11. The conference proceedings have been published in *Human Rights Law Journal* 2024, vol. 43, 2023, pp. 337 ff.

12. ECJ, C-565/19 P (Armando Carvalho), ECLI:EU:C:2021:252; and equally, CFI, T-330/18 (Armando Carvalho), ECLI:EU:T:2019:324.

13. The innovative approach of the European Court of Human Rights to the admissibility of the complaint by the "KlimaSeniorinnen Schweiz" group was particularly

surprising. In a rather daring legal development, the Court found their complaint admissible within the framework of an individual complaint under Art. 34 of the European Convention on Human Rights. For a comprehensive discussion of the Court's decision, see Christian Calliess and Niklas Täuber, "Klimaklagen nach dem Urteil des Europäischen Gerichtshofs für Menschenrechte" in *Neue Zeitschrift für Verwaltungsrecht*, 13, 2024, pp. 945 ff.; Julia Franziska Hänni, "Essentialia und Leitlinien für die Mitgliedstaaten des Europarates/Verein KlimaSeniorinnen gegen die Schweiz (EGMR-Urteil, 9. April 2024)" in *Europäische Grundrechte Zeitschrift* 2024, pp. 25 ff.

14. European Court of Human Rights, Judgment of April 9, 2024 - 53600/20 (Klimaseniorinnen/Schweiz), NVwZ 2024, 979.

15. The United Nations Framework Convention on Climate Change of May 9, 1992, United Nations, Treaty Series, vol. 1771, p. 107, came into force on March 21, 1994.

16. For further details, see Charlotte Blattner, "Warum das KlimaSeniorinnen-Urteil nicht undemokratisch ist," June 25, 2024, https://verfassungsblog.de/egmr-klimaseniorinnen-gewaltenteilung/ (accessed January 31, 2025).

17. Cf. The Federal Council's press release of August 28, 2024, https://www.admin.ch/gov/de/start/dokumentation/medienmitteilungen.msg-id-102244.html (accessed January 31, 2025).

CHAPTER 5

DEMOCRACY IN THE ANTHROPOCENE: HOW AND WHY THE END OF SECURITIES AFFECTS THE WAY WE LIVE AND GOVERN

CLAUDIA WIESNER

INTRODUCTION

This essay discusses the challenges that the Anthropocene—understood as both a new geological epoch and a questioning of modernity—poses for democracy, and it indicates some possible pathways for dealing with them. Building on my essays in the Convoco Editions of 2022 and 2023,[1] the aim is to link the current debates on the crisis of democracy and on the Anthropocene, which so far have remained largely disconnected: over the last few years, crisis diagnoses for representative democracy have been legion. There are several empirical indicators that underline decisive changes affecting representative democracy and its actors—citizens, politicians, civil society, parties, and governments. When seen in relation to the Anthropocene condition, the picture becomes much broader: the crisis symptoms and challenges reveal not only a crisis of democracy but a crisis of modernity and modern thinking altogether.

This diagnosis is far from being just a philosophical one: it has very concrete and very material consequences. We are facing entangled changes in the human and planetary condition which deeply affect the ways humans can live on the planet. The crisis symptoms of democracy are but one part in a large cluster of symptoms.

In this essay, I will briefly review the current crisis symptoms of representative democracy, then discuss what the "crisis of modernity" entails and how it is linked to the Anthropocene. This will be followed by a discussion of the challenges democracy faces in the Anthropocene, and possible ways of dealing with them.

This essay represents an interim stage of thinking on these matters, so it is a work in progress.

THE CRISIS SYMPTOMS OF DEMOCRACY REVISITED

As discussed at some length in my essay for the 2022 Convoco Edition, over the last few years crisis diagnoses for representative democracy have been legion. Several empirical indicators underline decisive changes affecting representative democracy, its context, and its actors—citizens, politicians, civil society, parties, and governments. Studies mention nine fields of democratic change that are pertinent.[2] The first six fields describe changes in how democracy works and manifests as such:

1) Democratic deconsolidation: pro-democratic attitudes are currently declining at least in a number of countries.[3]

2) Populism: populist parties and politicians have been on the rise worldwide; election results and support for populist parties have been increasing over the last few years in most established democracies.[4]

3) Democratic backsliding: in some representative democratic states, right-wing populist politicians have accessed government. In most of these states, the institutions and principles of representative democracy have been hollowed out.[5]

4) Technocracy: a number of current studies claim technocracy, i.e. decisions being shifted from democratically legitimized bodies to (more) opaque expert bodies, undermines representative democracy.[6]

5) Democratic innovations: a number of new tools and participatory mechanisms such as round tables or citizen budgets aim to enhance participation and stakeholder involvement, and hence trigger democratic activity.[7]

6) New movements: a number of new social movements on both left and right, such as the Indignados in Spain, Pegida in Germany, or the protest movements against climate change,[8] have been on the rise in the last decade. On the one hand, these new movements are a sign of democratic vitality, on the other hand, they do not necessarily always support representative democracy. Some even act openly against it, and not only the right-wing ones.

These changes in the actors and processes of representative democracy are accompanied by decisive changes in the societal context of democracy that can be summed up in three areas:

7) Two-thirds society: the tendency towards a two-thirds society is visible in a number of developed countries and has crucial effects on democratic participation, as lower social strata participate considerably less in democracy and society.[9]

8) Digitalization: understood as the process of using digitized information or data for business interests, digitalization entails a number of challenges to core democratic principles. The new currency of the digital age is no longer workforce or capital but data. Conceptions and practices of what an individual and what an individual's inalienable democratic and human rights are have changed, as have practices of government and public spaces. The latter have moved from national public spaces into different bubbles on social media.[10]

9) The globalization trilemma: formulated by Dani Rodrick,[11] the globalization trilemma states that out of three goals—namely democracy, high social

standards, and unlimited free trade—nation states can achieve only two. If a state opts for free trade, this comes at the expense of either national democratic standards or social standards. Liberal democracies in crisis have largely opted for participation in free trade, which has limited their margin of maneuver for maintaining democratic and social standards in times of (financial) crisis.

WHY IT IS NOT JUST ABOUT PHILOSOPHY: THE ANTHROPOCENE AND THE CRISIS OF MODERNITY

As mentioned in the introduction, when seen in relation to the Anthropocene condition, the crisis symptoms and challenges discussed above not only reveal a crisis of democracy, but a crisis of modernity and modern thinking altogether.

FROM CRISIS TO POLYCRISIS

The concept of crisis merits some discussion at this point. Both in Western academia and in public debates crisis diagnoses are many and "crisis talk" frequent. The labeling of complex problems such as climate change as "crisis," however, raises several questions. The concept of crisis is easily used as a catch-all concept, without proper definition and reflection, and in an inflationary manner. For over a decade, the EU has been at the center of crisis talk because it has struggled with a series of multiple and near-endless challenges: the financial crisis, the question of migration, Brexit, and most recently the COVID-19 pandemic and the war against Ukraine. Climate change is one of the main challenges on this list.

The accumulation of such "crises" can be read as just that—an accumulation of single crises that need to be overcome. But both academia and public debate have noted that they are linked to one another. The concept of "polycrisis," a term first invented by complexity theorists Edgar Morin and Anne Brigitte Kern,[12] tries to explain that we do not face single "crises" in isolation from others, but rather complex and entangled constellations of problems. The crises are linked, and they can accelerate each other.

But what is more, the crises also need to be seen and analyzed in relation to their context, historical background, and the complex factors that triggered them. They also need to be considered in a global and planetary perspective. In the EU, however, the crises at stake are too often discussed from a mainly EU-centered perspective, leaving out global entanglements and power relations when they are immediately relevant.

The ideational background of the crises is not touched upon either. There are not only related crises that add up to a polycrisis—the polycrisis is an outcome and a symptom of a crisis of modernity and modern thinking. It is, in other words, a symptom of the Anthropocene.

THE ANTHROPOCENE

The concept of the Anthropocene was coined in 2000[13] in the natural and Earth sciences. Today, it means first a new geological era. Several natural scientists have argued that about seventy years ago Earth left the Holocene and entered the Anthropocene, a period in which human-induced changes mark the planet decisively. Humans not only impacted so much on nature that it changed decisively, they are also affected by these changes in return. Climate change is not the only important effect but the most visible and maybe the most dangerous one. Humans have to face up to the fact that they are part of nature themselves.

Second, the Anthropocene indicates a challenge to modern thinking and the modern worldview or ontology. This means that the changing global, human, and natural condition challenges modern conceptions of both knowledge and agency[14] or, to put it bluntly, what used to work in the last few decades does not work anymore. Concretely, this not only refers to the tools of governance we are used to, it means a whole way of life and thinking: If humans continue to impact nature, nature will continue to change, and this will affect humans negatively. If humans continue to exploit nature and live in non-sustainable ways, they will limit their own resources for life and ultimately imperil human life itself. In consequence, humans have to change their way of life and their way of thinking about nature and the planet. In a nutshell, humans have to rethink the modern way of living and thinking if they want to survive and develop new tools to deal with the crises.

This idea is far from new: it has been discussed at least since the books published by the Club of Rome that came out in the 1970s and 1980s, and it has been more and more generally recognized. The United Nations took up the challenge a long time ago too, with the first UN Climate Conference taking place in 1979 in Geneva. But the changes that followed have been slow and the steps too small. The most pertinent Anthropocene problem, climate change, has had such a decisive impact that today it affects everyday life more and more severely, to the point that it is difficult to still negate it.

The Anthropocene is thus not just created by new problems that arise, it is not just a series of crises, and not even a polycrisis. The concept encompasses several parts of the problem: what we call the "polycrisis", the crisis of modern thinking, and the ensuing inability to solve the crises through traditional ways of governing. The Anthropocene emphasizes not only the changes the planet faces, but also the limits of traditional knowledge assumptions, of linear causality, and of universal applicability.

The challenge is thus fundamental. We not only face a series of crises, but also a crisis of thinking about the new problems and of acting to tackle them, since established knowledge assumptions reach their limits facing non-linear and non-causal problems. Hence, the problem we have to tackle is as much a crisis of understanding, knowledge, and finding ways of tackling new problem constellations. In a more contingent and uncertain world, policy knowledge needs to be rethought. These new problems cannot be dealt with using traditional frameworks of understanding. We are facing a changing constellation of material reality and the knowledge about it, in which our established ways of living in and thinking about the world, and of governing it, no longer work.

All in all, it is not simply a crisis that is at stake, nor just several crises, or a polycrisis, but a deep-rooted questioning of the bases of our societies and economies, i.e. of liberal modernity itself in the Anthropocene. As we will now discuss, these words are certainly not only, nor even mainly, to be understood in philosophical terms. They have a very concrete and very material meaning for our societies and for democracy.

DEMOCRACY IN THE ANTHROPOCENE

The Anthropocene and its symptoms directly affect modern societies in a very concrete sense. For one, the fact that the planet's ecological and geological systems are becoming increasingly unstable and vulnerable directly affects humans and their lives all over the world, as well as increasingly at the heart of the liberal order—floods, heatwaves, or hurricanes are appearing in areas that have been exempt from natural disasters for decades or even centuries. Moreover, as discussed above, besides climate change, Western states in the last decade have also been dealing with the direct and quite material consequences of the financial crisis, migration waves, the pandemic, and the war against Ukraine. This series of entangled crises has triggered the changes to democracy outlined at the beginning.

Experiencing this series of immediate threats and blows has triggered citizens' doubts about the legitimacy of their governments, states, and the EU. Citizens have openly questioned them because in their concrete experience both their individual capacities to deal with the crisis symptoms and the collective capacities of their societies and governments to do so were limited. There have been protests in reaction, but there also have been new movements—one of the most prominent is the Fridays for Future movement, in which young people demonstrated in favor of government action to limit climate change.

Governments, however, have not remained passive in the face of the challenges of the Anthropocene. Most governments have begun to accelerate their reactions and strategies to combat climate change. Western states in particular are trying to cut down on industries and infrastructures that consume natural resources, invest in renewable energies, and support sustainable transformations. The EU tackled the financial crisis with austerity and rescue packages,

it tried to reduce migration, and European governments even aimed at finding common responses to the
COVID-19 pandemic and the war against Ukraine.
But despite these endeavors, governments' abilities to
take control of the complex and entangled problems
of the Anthropocene remain very limited.

A fundamental question is thus whether representative democracies and their governments can tackle
the Anthropocene challenges at all. At this point, a
quadruple challenge for democracies emerges.

First, as we noted above, established modes of
governance and democracy no longer work "as they
used to" or "as they should." This is because in the
Anthropocene two core ideas of modern thinking are
questioned: the idea of a separation between humans/
culture and nature, and the idea of linearity and simple
causality in human action and in politics. Instead, we
have to face up to the fact that all life on the planet
functions in complex systems and entanglements
that models of causality and linearity fail to grasp.
Governance is no longer simple or a matter of rational
control and regulation; it does not follow linear
causality schemes (if it ever did). The consequences in
terms of the perception of democratic governance are
critical enough, in a literal sense: Established mechanisms of governance no longer working means, to put

it bluntly, that democratic governments cannot deliver policy output as they used too, or maybe even that they openly and outrightly fail to control a complex problem. This experience is, of course, a major trigger of public dissatisfaction.

Second, if we want to tackle the challenges of the Anthropocene, huge transformations are needed in modern societies. The transformations that are necessary to change modern societies to sustainable ones are not only huge, but the related costs of transformation are huge too. The question of who is going to pay for the transformations, or who suffers from them, is crucial. Expressed in a concrete example this means that if German coal mining companies stop coal mining in Germany this is surely a move in favor of ecological sustainability, but it is almost as surely a move against social sustainability in the coal region, if the transformation is carried out too quickly and without any complementing measures that create alternative professional futures for thousands of coal workers. If governments aim for such complementary measures, the budget for them needs to be gained first. Buffering the consequences of transformation is costly.

Third, liberal democracy is itself a complex and demanding system of governance. For good reason, there are checks and balances and majority-based decision-making procedures. One main reason behind this is that a reflective, transparent, and public exchange of arguments, of the pros and cons,[15] of an issue or a decision at stake, increases public understanding and legitimacy of the ensuing decisions instead of simply forcing them on people. These procedures are without alternative in liberal democracies. But the duration of the necessary deliberations and procedures can contradict claims for "immediate action" or "the one truth about climate change." Moreover, liberal democracy is based on the demos as sovereign, and on plurality,[16] not on single and isolated voices. A plurality of interests has to be represented, a plurality of voices to be heard. Representative democracy thus aims at listening to the plurality of voices in the demos, and not "to science", as a famous slogan by the Fridays for Future movement claims. This means that we have to cope with both the duration of democratic processes and the fact that citizens disagree, interests have to be balanced, and compromises have to be found, if we want to govern the Anthropocene democratically. To listen only, or mainly, "to science" would be quite simply undemocratic.

Fourth, the social and cultural effects of transformation have so far been underestimated. A concrete consequence of the Anthropocene setting, of the manifold crises that are interlinked, has been to trigger feelings of vulnerability, precariousness, and uncertainty. Many people are quite simply afraid of the threats and changes ahead and feel insecure. Climate change is often linked to imaginaries of decay, loss of control, or even apocalypse[17] that also concern the centers of Western liberal democracy.[18] The series of other "crises" adds up to this. But the threat does not only lie in the fear of apocalypse. The transformations that are necessary if climate change is to be limited will also change established ways of life, and thus their prospect threatens economic, social, and cultural securities. Citizens as well as companies all over the world are concretely and economically threatened by the transformations ahead. Moreover, some people experience the necessary transformations as impertinent, since they will interfere with their habits and status. A considerable number of people seem to adopt positions in which they deny or contradict the changes or the necessity of transformation by, for example, denying climate change, whether because they avoid seeing the real dangers, or because the necessary transformations represent a threat to their habits, traditions, or status. Populist parties are often very good at taking up these resentments. A prominent case are politicians who simply deny that climate change is taking place, but there are also arguments that claim to defend individual habits, cultures, or traditions. The most recent German election campaigns featured slogans such as "Don't touch my Schnitzel!" or "No kind of heating is illegal." These slogans criticize government projects that propose limiting the consumption of industrially produced meat or changing the type of heating in domestic housing.

WHAT CAN BE DONE?

What, then, can be done if we want to safeguard democracy in the Anthropocene? There are quite a few challenges ahead, ranging from tackling the changes of democracy outlined at the beginning, via an ecological transformation of world societies in order to deal with climate change and other crises and developing a sustainable, truly "postmodern" way of governance, to balancing different interests and power imbalances, tackling concrete conflicts, and developing a more equal world. To call this complex and demanding is a huge understatement. The following discussion outlines some initial thoughts on what the dangers are, but also possible ways forward. The first two points discuss the dangers of technocratic approaches and expertise, which will probably not work very well and moreover intensify the crisis of democracy.

First, as discussed in the 2024 Convoco Edition, "more of the same" will most probably not be enough or even helpful in tackling the challenges of the Anthropocene.[19] The current answers to the crisis scenarios, whether at EU level or beyond, for example, via the United Nations, often advocate resilience and/or anticipatory governance, searching for pathways and mechanisms that equip modern governance in such a way as to make it resilient to the challenges. In many policy papers by the EU, the UN, or the OECD, the Anthropocene challenges of climate change, security, new technologies, or artificial intelligence are dealt with as complex policy fields—adding more complexity than ever before—that accordingly require more complex and more expert-based mechanisms of governance, more technocracy, more control, and more bureaucracy. This also means that the Anthropocene challenges are divided into separate clusters or policy fields and controlled by expertise and bureaucracy. But, in short, more chaos cannot be countered by more control. It is questionable whether such approaches can really manage complex problems, i.e. whether they really can provide answers to the scenario of entangled challenges. Most of the respective approaches still rely largely on the modern, rationalist, linear, and expertise-oriented way of governing, offering just more of the same. Instead of seeing one cause and one effect, they now aim at several causes and several effects, but remain linear.

Second, expertise and technocracy intensify the problems of democracy because, in short, they bring more depoliticization and less democracy. As discussed in the last Convoco Edition,[20] crisis reactions sometimes operate at the expense of thick modes of legitimation. Moreover, expert-based modes of governance often reduce the impact of democratically legitimized fora of deliberation and decision-making such as parliaments,[21] and this entails a reduction in public debate and transparency, because experts usually discuss behind closed doors. New bureaucratic requirements also increase the workloads of people who have to deal with the new forms and formalities, and they tend to increase citizens' distance from the bureaucratic and technocratic world of "those above," hence triggering criticism of democracy.

This means that technocratic and expert-oriented solutions will most probably intensify the crisis of democracy in the Anthropocene. In contrast, the following points three to six sketch possible pathways and steps to take in order to enable the democratic governance of the Anthropocene, ranging from the most concrete level of political action to principled and normative questions.

Third, and in practice in the Western democracies, it seems wise to start facing the challenges ahead by trusting the potential of debate. Not explaining and not discussing difficult issues such as the needs of an ecological transformation—be it in a coal region or with regard to changes to the ways of heating individual buildings—will obviously not help people understand the needs that lie behind or support the related policies. For many people the related fears, as we said above, are as concrete as the economic threats. Fears cannot be remedied by not taking them into account or downplaying them, but they can be tackled by open debate, and by people seeing concrete positive effects, i.e. by policy output.

Fourth, governance in the Anthropocene needs to be rethought and to change, taking into account that there is no simple relationship of cause and effect, and no action without unintended consequences, including the fact that we cannot fully know what the cascade of effects of an action will be. Anthropocene modes of governance need to positively embrace complexity and opacity, i.e. the fact that the world is organized in complex systems and that we cannot know all the effects of actions or events in advance. Approaches based on quantum theory or chaos theory take this into account[22] and could be a basis for rethinking governance in the Anthropocene.

Fifth, the economic consequences of ecological transformation need to be remedied in order to prevent people losing their jobs, their houses, or their complete social structure. This will require ecological investment in people and infrastructure as well as transfer payments (whichever form they take in the end). In combination with open debate and thus—hopefully—the broadening of public support, a developing ecological infrastructure can trigger people's positive reception of the transformation. As a concrete example, if Germany had a broad, efficient, well-priced, and coherently networked public transport system with smooth connections between high-speed trains and local transport in the countryside, plus a good supply of affordable ecological cars to complement this, the benefits of an ecological transformation away from fuel cars would be much more visible and appreciated.

Sixth, there is a huge conceptual challenge ahead. The Anthropocene does not mean abandoning democracy, but it means rethinking it, most probably decisively. There are manifold questions of a normative, theoretical, and practical character: What about more-than-humans, i.e. do we need to include animals and plants into our democratic decision-making systems, and what about the planet as a whole? How should we tackle questions about ecological justice and climate justice and global inequalities? How can we make societies sustainable?

Nothing of the above is absolutely impossible. On the contrary, all of these steps can be taken, thought through, and put into practice.

Notes

1. Claudia Wiesner, "Democratic Equality and Changes in Modern Liberal Democracies" in Corinne M. Flick (ed.), *Equality in an Unequal World* (Munich: Convoco Editions, 2023); Claudia Wiesner, "Relations, Networks, and Entanglements: The Anthropocene as a Challenge to Modern Democratic Governance in Europe" in Corinne M. Flick (ed.), *Is the Open Society Sustainable in Case of Emergency?* (Munich: Convoco Editions, 2024).

2. Wiesner, "Democratic Equality and Changes in Modern Liberal Democracies"; Claudia Wiesner "The War Against Ukraine, the Changing World Order and the Conflict Between Democracy and Autocracy" in Claudia Wiesner and Michèle Knodt (eds.), *The War Against Ukraine and the EU: Facing New Realities* (Cham, Switzerland: Springer Nature, 2024), pp. 83–109.

3. Amy Alexander and Christian Welzel, "The Myth of Deconsolidation: Rising Liberalism and the Populist Reaction" in *Journal of Democracy* (2017); Roberto Stefan Fao and Yascha Mounk, "The End of the Consolidation Paradigm: A Response to Our Critics" in *Journal of Democracy* (2017); Pippa Norris, "Is Western Democracy Backsliding? Diagnosing the Risks" in *Journal of Democracy* (2017), https://www.journalofdemocracy.org/online-exchange-democratic-deconsolidation/ (accessed December 16, 2024).

4. Daniele Albertazzi and Duncan McDonnell, *Twenty-First Century Populism: The Spectre of Western European Democracy* (London: Palgrave Macmillan, 2008); Nadia Urbinati, *Me the People: How Populism Transforms Democracy* (Cambridge, MA: Harvard University Press, 2019).

5. Nancy Bermeo, "On Democratic Backsliding" in *Journal of Democracy* 27 (1) (2016), pp. 5–19, https://doi.org/10.1353/jod.2016.0012; Steven Levitsky and Daniel Ziblatt, *How Democracies Die* (New York: Crown, 2018).

6. Nadia Urbinati, *Democracy Disfigured: Opinion, Truth, and the People* (Cambridge, MA/ London: Harvard University Press, 2014).

7. Brigitte Geissel and Marko Joas, *Participatory Democratic Innovations in Europe: Improving the Quality of Democracy?* (Leverkusen: Barbara Budrich Publishers, 2013).

8. Christian Volk, "Zwischen Entpolitisierung Und Radikalisierung – Zur Theorie Von Demokratie Und Politik in Zeiten Des Widerstands" in *Politische Vierteljahresschrift* 54 (1) (2013), pp. 75–110, https://www.jstor.org/stable/24201175?seq=1#page_scan_tab_contentshttps://www.nomos-elibrary.de/10.5771/0032-3470-2013-1-75/zwischen-entpolitisierung-und-radikalisierung-zur-theorie-von-demokratie-und-politik-in-zeiten-des-widerstands-jahrgang-54-2013-heft-1 (accessed December 9, 2024).

9. Arlie Russell Hochschild, *Strangers in Their Own Land: Anger and Mourning on the American Right* (New York/London: The New Press, 2018); Claudia Wiesner, *Multi-Level-Governance und lokale Demokratie: Politikinnovationen im Vergleich* (Wiesbaden: Springer VS, 2017).

10. Shoshana Zuboff, *The Age of Surveillance Capitalism: The Fight for a Human Future at the New Frontier of Power* (New York: Public Affairs, 2019); Evgeny Morozov, *To Save Everything, Click Here: The Folly of Technological Solutionism* (New York: Public Affairs/Perseus Books, 2013).

11. Dani Rodrik, *The Globalization Paradox: Democracy and the Future of the World Economy* (New York: W.W. Norton & Company, 2011).

12. Michael Lawrence, "Polycrisis in the Anthropocene: An Invitation to Contributions and Debates" in *Global Sustainability* 7:e5 (2024), https://doi.org/10.1017/sus.2024.2; Michael Lawrence, et al., "Global Polycrisis: The Causal Mechanisms of Crisis Entanglement" in *Global Sustainability* 7:e6 (2024).

13. Paul J. Crutzen and Eugene F. Stoermer, "The 'Anthropocene' (2000)" in Susanne Benner et al. (eds.), *Paul J. Crutzen and the Anthropocene: A New Epoch in Earth's History* (Cham, Switzerland: Springer, 2021), pp. 19–21.

14. See, for example, David Chandler, Franziska Müller, and Delf Rothe (eds.), *International Relations in the Anthropocene* (Cham, Switzerland: Springer Nature, 2021).

15. Kari Palonen, *Parliamentary Thinking: Procedure, Rhetoric and Time* (Cham, Switzerland: Springer International Publishing, 2019).

16. Nadia Urbinati, *Representative Democracy. Principles and Genealogy* (Chicago, IL: University of Chicago Press, 2006); Urbinati, *Democracy Disfigured: Opinion, Truth, and the People.*

17. See, for example, Anna Lowenhaupt Tsing, *The Mushroom at the End of the World: On the Possibility of Life in Capitalist Ruins* (Princeton/Oxford: Princeton University Press, 2021).

18. Bruno Latour, *Down to Earth: Politics in the New Climatic Regime* (Cambridge: Polity Press, 2018).

19. Wiesner, "Relations, Networks, and Entanglements."

20. Ibid.

21. Claudia Wiesner, *Inventing the EU as a Democratic Polity: Concepts, Actors and Controversies* (Cham, Switzerland: Springer Science and Business Media/Palgrave Macmillan, 2019), pp. 281–301; Claudia Wiesner, "Representative Democracy in Financial Crisis Governance: New Challenges in the EU Multi-level System" in Diane Fromage and Anna Herranz-Suralles (eds.), *Executive-Legislative (Im)balance in the European Union* (London: Bloomsbury Publishing, 2021), pp. 227–44.

22. James Der Derian and Alexander Wendt (eds.), *Quantum International Relations: A Human Science for World Politics* (Oxford: Oxford University Press, 2022).

CHAPTER 6

DOES THE CONCEPT OF THE SOCIAL MARKET ECONOMY OFFER A SUITABLE FRAMEWORK FOR ECONOMIC POLICY OF THE FUTURE?

CLEMENS FUEST

I. INTRODUCTION

In light of the complex, major challenges facing the attempt to create a future that is free, just, and sustainable, the question arises whether current forms of shaping social and political processes need to be changed, or whether we can hold onto them. In Germany, the concept of the social market economy is probably the most widely accepted form of economic policy. This is doubtless down to the fact that the concept is somewhat vague. Depending on their preference, different people emphasize the social aspect or the market aspect. Despite or precisely because of this vagueness, the social market economy plays an important role in debates about how to deal with current economic and political challenges. On the one hand such debates call repeatedly for politicians to "return" to the principles of the social market economy, while on the other hand, it is argued that in light of new challenges, the idea of the social market economy must be developed, changed, or even abandoned altogether. Against this backdrop, this essay discusses whether and, if so, in what way the concept of the social market economy can and should continue to provide a framework for economic policy in the future.

II. THE ECONOMIC BACKGROUND TO THE CONCEPT OF THE SOCIAL MARKET ECONOMY

The concept of the social market economy is not a self-contained theoretical structure, but a series of economic and socio-political ideas that have been put forward by various authors, including Walter Eucken,

Alfred Müller-Armack, and Wilhelm Röpke.[1] The concept was developed against the backdrop of the crises that emerged during the first half of the 20th century and in light of the task of reconstruction after World War II, and served as an important benchmark for economic policy in Germany. Its core is the competitive order that is based on private property, freedom of contract, free pricing mechanisms, and an active competition policy to prevent the abuse of market power.

The concept of the social market economy aims primarily to achieve a high degree of economic efficiency through market-based pricing control, including a supply of goods that is oriented towards individual, heterogeneous preferences. This is the economic efficiency of the social market economy. In addition, it also pursues the goal of a broad-based participation in prosperity. This is the meaning of "social" in the social market economy.

Market-based competition itself is a major factor in ensuring that the population can share in prosperity. Effective competition ensures that goods are not offered at excessive prices. Monopolies reduce production volumes, thus worsening supply and increasing prices. The owners of the monopolies profit at the expense of the rest of society, and overall economic efficiency falls. A lack of competition in the labor market in the form of labor demand monopolies means that employers can drive down wages. If this is combined with a reduction in the volume of work, production quantities fall and prices of the goods produced rise. However, trade unions can also monopolize the supply of labor and drive up wages, which can then equally lead to underemployment. In this case, those in work profit at the expense of those who cannot get a job at such high wages. The quantity of goods produced falls and prices rise.

However, the social aspect affects not only the quantities and prices of goods and services and the level of wages. This aspect of the concept also includes social security, i.e. protection against risks such as sickness, unemployment, or occupational disability. Providing insurance against these risks can, to a certain extent, become the individual's own responsibility, for example through savings or private insurance. Where personal provision reaches its limits, the state can step in to add cover. The boundary between private and state risk provision is one of the central topics in social policy debates.

Another aspect of the social side of the social market economy concerns distribution and redistribution goals beyond protection against general risks in life such as sickness or occupational disability. This includes, for example, the distribution of burdens in the tax system, for example through the implementation of progressive income tax. The "classical" literature on the social market economy does not deal very much with the specific design of the tax system. However, it does demand that taxation should not disrupt the competitive order any more than is unavoidable, i.e., above all, it should distort price signals as little as possible. A certain degree of negative impact in the form of a distortion of relative prices is unavoidable and concerns the fact that taxation is not just about raising tax revenue, but also about distributing the tax burden according to current principles of justice. For example, the idea that people with higher incomes should pay more taxes means that the price ratio between consumption and leisure is distorted.

In addition, literature on the social market economy and regulatory policy includes an extensive discussion of state economic policy's potential fields of intervention in the areas of short-term economic policy, environmental policy, education policy, and foreign trade. Political intervention in these areas can conflict with the market system and competitive order that are fundamental to the social market economy. But it can also be implemented in such a way that these conflicts are avoided or kept within narrow limits. One important criterion for this is that the interventions are compatible with the market. Wilhelm Röpke defines market compatibility as follows: "Interventions which do not interfere with the price mechanism and with the automatism of the market derived from it are compatible, they let themselves be absorbed as new 'data'; interventions which paralyse the price mechanism and therefore force us to replace it by a planned (collectivist) order, we call incompatible" (Röpke, 1992, p. 160; quoted in Barth, 2011, p. 13).

The criterion of market compatibility can be applied to many areas of economic policy. For example, it implies that rent controls in the form of maximum rents should be rejected because they eliminate the control function of rents and exacerbate housing shortages. Instead, personalized support in the form of housing benefits is preferable. State interventions designed to maintain or intelligently use market conditions, up to and including the creation of markets using prices to signal scarcity where none previously existed, play a role in various contexts, especially in environmental and climate policy.

III. THE DEVELOPMENT POTENTIAL OF THE CONCEPT OF THE SOCIAL MARKET ECONOMY

The concept of the social market economy was developed against the backdrop of reconstruction after the devastation of World War II and the inter-system competition between the centrally planned economies of the Eastern bloc and the market economy systems of the West, and it influenced Germany's economic policy during this time. This raises the question of how relevant the concept remains today. The competition between economic systems has long been decided in favor of the market economy. At the same time, the world's dominant market-oriented economic systems and their associated economic policy are facing new challenges. These include the globalization of the economy, global environmental problems, demographic change, increasing inequality of income and wealth in some countries, accelerating technological change including digitalization, new geopolitical tensions and, last but not least, the political polarization observed in some Western democracies, and the growing influence of populist political forces.

III.1 THE HISTORICAL DEVELOPMENT OF THE
CONCEPT OF THE SOCIAL MARKET ECONOMY

The development potential of the concept of the social market economy was a subject that engaged the very people who coined the term. For example, Müller-Armack states: "After a trial period, every program of economic policy requires critical review with regard to what has been achieved and what is to be achieved in the future." (Müller-Armack, 1960/1966, p. 267). Thus, even in the early 1960s, he was describing a "second phase of the social market economy" (see also Müller-Armack, 1962/1966).[2] Müller-Armack said that in the 1950s the social market economy had proved successful in a first phase whose the aim was to solve basic supply problems to improve social conditions, to achieve full employment, and generally to achieve stable economic development. Now a new phase was beginning: "We must [...] assume that the social market economy [...] is entering a second phase in which, while continuing everything that has been started, a new emphasis must be placed on the whole" (Müller-Armack, 1960, p. 303). What does this mean? "This [...] refers to the observation that aims of the past, especially those of overcoming scarcity [...] are fading away. It is success itself that makes much of what has been achieved seem self-evident" (ibid., p. 310). Müller-Armack (1962) discusses the tasks and economic and sociopolitical challenges that arise in this second phase of the social market economy. Among them he includes the growing importance of the "environment as a whole in which the individual lives in industrial society." On the one hand, these are aspects of the working environment in companies, which include accident prevention and health protection in the workplace; on the other hand, they include environmental policy issues in the ecological sense, i.e. concerns such as "maintaining clean air and water" (ibid., p. 280) and the establishment of nature reserves. This area also includes aspects of infrastructure development, regional planning, and urban development, as well as dealing with technological progress and structural change, which today includes coal mines, for example, that are confronted with the expansion of oil and gas as energy sources, as well as the rise of nuclear energy.

How can the concept of the social market economy contribute to solving these new challenges? Müller-Armack does not regard the concept as a fixed set of rigid principles, but rather as a "style of behavior in our world that aspires to a certain kind of solution to social problems" (Müller-Armack, 1960, p. 299). How does that work? The starting point is the idea that individuals and groups that make up society pursue a "magic triangle of goals" that consists of personal freedom, economic growth, and economic and social security. These goals are sometimes in conflict with one another, and different groups place very different emphasis on these goals. The social market economy is a "stylistic formula that attempts to bring the [...] goals [...] into a practical balance. [...] The social market economy is thus a formula for integration that attempts to bring the essential forces of our present-day society into genuine cooperation" (Müller-Armack, 1962).

By contrast with the radical approaches of market liberalism on the one hand or state interventionism on the other, which do not balance each other out, the social market economy acts to this end as a compromise technique. The social market economy is therefore understood as a flexible concept. This flexibility should not, however, be confused with an economic policy that "seeks salvation in legislative amendments and day-to-day politics" (ibid., p. 310). This means that it is important not to lose sight of economic regulatory circumstances, which imply, for example, that market-compatible interventions create different effects from interventions that are not market-compatible.

III.2 SOCIAL MARKET ECONOMY, ORDOLIBERALISM, AND AN EVIDENCE-BASED APPROACH

In more recent debates about economic policy, the concepts of ordoliberalism and the social market economy have been criticized for placing too little emphasis on evidence-based economic policy decisions and for being too dogmatic (see, for example, the debate in Fuest et al., 2006). This aspect is particularly important for the issue of the development of the concept. Interestingly, the understanding of the early proponents of the social market economy and ordoliberalism is quite different. They rejected ideological debates about economic policy (Röpke, 1950, p. 9, calls it a "carnival of ideologies") and demanded that economic policy be based not only on theoretical considerations but also on empirical evidence. Eucken describes this as follows:

> We could and should finally move from the stage of speculation to enter the stage of experience-based economic policy. We can draw upon considerable experiences in the areas of monetary policies, crisis policies, agricultural policies, cartel policies, trading policies, tax policies and the like etc. Indeed, these experiences ought to be exhausted; selective descriptions are not sufficient (Eucken, 1952/1990, p. 15).

He also considers lessons learned from other periods of economic history to be central: "Humankind could have learned much from 150 years of industrialization, which developed in various countries using very different methods. But a mixture of slogans and outdated ideologies lies like a haze over reality." (Eucken, 1952/1990), p. 19.) Hence his demand: "And the only chance of overcoming the systemic problem is to exploit this experience, focus on the objective, and renounce the ideologies of the past." (Eucken, 1952/1990), p. 19.) Accordingly, we can say that evidence-based economic policy decisions belong to the intellectual tradition of the social market economy. It should go without saying that this includes advances in methods and data availability. Whether this has always been adequately reflected in practical economic policy and economic policy advice is another matter.

IV. GLOBALIZATION AND THE VARIOUS FORMS OF INTER-SYSTEM COMPETITION

The concept of the social market economy assigns to the state the task of shaping the framework for private sector activity. However, state activity still takes place largely at the level of nation states. Supranational alliances such as the European Union or international institutions such as the World Trade Organization, the International Monetary Fund, the OECD, or the United Nations play an important role. However, we cannot say that they have replaced the national level in the role of shaping economic policy or that such a development is in prospect. Economic policy is still primarily the job of nation states.

By contrast, economic activity today is extremely international. Goods, services, capital, and labor are increasingly mobile across borders. This has consequences for national economic policies. The cross-border mobility of economic activity has far-reaching consequences for political activity. As a result of this mobility, the nation state, which people expect to set the framework for private-sector competition, is itself under competitive pressure. Competition between states arises—including their economic policies—which is also referred to as inter-system competition. Clearly, we must explain whether and how the concept of the social market economy functions under these conditions of inter-system competition.

IV.1 INTER-SYSTEM COMPETITION BETWEEN CENTRALLY PLANNED ECONOMIES AND MARKET ECONOMIES

The competition triggered by cross-border mobility is basically nothing new in that it already shaped the "first inter-system competition," i.e. the competition between Communist centrally planned economies and Western market economies. In divided Germany, but also in other parts of the world, people *en masse* voted with their feet in the early phases of this inter-system competition. Millions of people left the GDR, preferring to live in the Federal Republic of Germany. Other Communist states, such as Cuba, experienced similar waves of emigration. Of course, the East German government tried to avoid this competitive pressure by building the Wall, just as other Communist states made it difficult or impossible for their citizens to leave the country. Ultimately, the desire of many people to leave the GDR was undeniable proof of the inferiority of the socialist economic system and a decisive factor in its collapse. From the perspective of the concept of the social market economy, this inter-system competition only proved that the more humane system prevailed. This corresponds to the analysis and predictions of the early philosophers of the social market economy, who denounced Communism and centrally planned economies, including their concept of humanity, as inhumane (for example, Röpke, 1958).

IV.2 GLOBALIZATION AND COMPETITION BETWEEN MARKET ECONOMIES

A second form of inter-system competition is the competition between market-oriented states with democratic and constitutional political systems, which is also driven by cross-border mobility of economic activity. From the perspective of the concept of the social market economy and its notions of regulation, it is reasonable to assume that this competition between states, like private-sector competition, requires a competitive order that prevents large, powerful states, for example, from abusing their market power at the expense of other states. At the same time, economic integration itself depends on economic policy resolutions, such as decisions about the liberalization of capital movements or joining trade agreements.

The mobility of economic activity puts national economic policy itself under competitive pressure. Investors, workers, and taxpayers can "vote with their feet" and react to differences in the attractiveness of countries and locations. This competition is evaluated very differently in the economic literature. Analogous to private sector competition, Charles Tiebout (1956) sees competition between regional authorities as advantageous because, according to his analysis, this competition ensures that citizens are provided with public services that match with their individual preferences. George Zodrow and Peter Mieszkowski (1986) counter that such competition between regional authorities can lead to inefficiencies if the state has to resort to instruments that cause economic distortions in order to do its job. Using the financing of public goods as an example, they show that the use of distorting taxes in tax competition can lead to a shortage of public goods. The basic problem is that while individual governments recognize the consequences of their actions as regards their own population, they neglect their impact on the economies of other countries. Hans-Werner Sinn (2002) argues along the same lines and counters the thesis of efficient interstate competition by saying that the state takes action precisely in areas where private-sector competition does not operate, i.e. in cases of market failure. Therefore, he claims, the introduction of competition between states does not lead to benefits but to a loss of prosperity (similarly from a legal perspective, see Paul Kirchhof, 2004).

The basic problem with this position, which fundamentally rejects interstate competition, is the underlying premise that national governments always create optimal conditions for economic activity or always ensure an optimal supply of public goods. This premise must necessarily lead to the conclusion that restricting state scope for action through competition cannot improve overall economic prosperity. Analogously, private-sector competition cannot lead to better results than the central planning of economic activity if the central planner has all the incentives and information required to implement optimal allocation of resources for the economy as a whole. As Viktor Vanberg (2005) explains in responding to Kirchhof (2004), the function of competition as a process of incentives, disempowerment, and discovery also applies in principle to states, even if the effect differs in detail from the effect of competition in private-sector markets. The literature on tax competition shows, for example, that tax coordination, as stipulated by theories that assume benevolent and omniscient governments, can reduce the welfare of citizens, in light of imperfections in the political process.

Of course, this does not yet answer the question of what a competitive order for states should look like and what guidance the concept of the social market economy can provide for the economic policy of a country that is exposed to such competition.

IV.3 THE THIRD TYPE OF INTER-SYSTEM COMPETITION AND GEOECONOMICS

The rise of China and geopolitical tensions between China and the US have given rise to a new form of inter-system competition between democracies and more or less market-based but politically authoritarian states such as China, which can be described as the "third type of inter-system competition" (Fuest, 2018). Alongside geopolitical tensions, this also involves the question of whether an economic system with market-economy elements but an authoritarian political system can keep up with or even surpass the systems prevailing in the West that combine market economy, democracy, and the rule of law. The geopolitical tensions that have risen sharply as a result of Russia's attack on Ukraine are overshadowing global economic relations and underscoring the risks that can go hand-in-hand with international economic dependencies. Governments can use economic power for geopolitical purposes. This calls into question the model of rules-based, free global trade.

The concept of the social market economy raises the question of whether and how it can serve as a framework in a world that is more profoundly defined by geopolitical conflicts. At the very least, the concept reminds us that abandoning a more or less rule-based international system of trade is associated with considerable economic disadvantages. It also reminds us that the fact of others violating these rules, for example by applying tariffs or trade-distorting subsidies, does not automatically mean that Germany or the EU should abandon these rules too.

V. GLOBAL ENVIRONMENTAL PROBLEMS

Global warming, the decline in biodiversity, pollution, overfishing of the world's oceans, and the shrinking of natural habitats require changes in the way we do business. Environmental policy plays a central role in the social market economy in that the internalization of external effects is one of the basic ways in which prices adequately reflect scarcity. In the historical development of the concept of the social market economy, environmental issues have become more important over time. However, solving local and national environmental problems poses challenges that differ from those involved in solving global environmental problems. In addition, the population's interest in ecological sustainability is growing as living standards rise. The importance of ecological challenges is also made clear by the fact that some political parties no longer refer to the social market economy but rather to the eco-social market economy. The ecological sustainability of economic activity has joined the classical goals of increasing prosperity and broad-based participation. The goal of decarbonizing the economy pursued within the framework of climate policy is such a far-reaching and profound change that the term "transformation" is being used, a term that was previously used primarily for the transition from centrally planned economies to a market economy after the fall of the Iron Curtain in 1989.

Analogous to the "second phase of the social market economy" as cited above (Müller-Armack, 1962/1966), we could also say that the concept of the social market economy is now to be understood as a "stylistic formula" for finding a balance between these new goals in practice, without ideologically driven radicalism. Criteria for instruments such as market compatibility also offer relevant frameworks here, but must be examined critically to see whether they remain appropriate in light of the new conditions and objectives.

VI. CONCLUSION

The concept of the social market economy was not intended by those who coined the phrase to be a self-contained guide to economic policy, but as a policy style, i.e. an open process that attempts to use the benefits of the market economy to create prosperity in the interests of a broad majority of the population. This policy style means recognizing that different individuals and groups evaluate and assess different social goals in different ways. It also means recognizing that goals and their assessment can change over time. In addition, these goals may conflict with each other. Such conflicts exist, for example, between the goal of having an efficient and dynamic economy and the goal of protecting individuals as comprehensively as possible against unemployment, illness, or poverty in old age.

It is perhaps asking a bit much to expect the writings of the intellectual fathers of the social market economy to give us guidance on how economic policy should address current challenges such as climate change or globalization. The requirement, which was already relevant in the early years, to reject radical or ideological approaches to economic policy, to be open to learning from experience, to limit the influence of interest groups, and to be willing to compromise, has nevertheless retained its relevance to this day.

Notes

1. The concept of the social market economy originates with Alfred Müller-Armack (1946/1990).

2. Surely the question is whether the economic policy of the 1950s in Germany can actually be seen at least in part as an implementation of the concept of the social market economy. Müller-Armack (1978, p. 326) himself writes: "What is the social market economy? In the first place it is an economic order of a market economy, as not yet realized in history." By contrast, Goldschmidt and Kolev (2023, p. 11) postulate that the social market economy is "the economic and social system that was established in West Germany after World War II."

Bibliography

Veronica Barth, *Die Soziale Marktwirtschaft: Ideen der Gründerväter und praktische Umsetzung* (Gütersloh: Bertelsmann-Stiftung, 2011).

Walter Eucken, *Grundsätze der Wirtschaftspolitik*, 6th edn. (Tübingen: Mohr, 1952/1990).

Clemens Fuest, "Internationale Koordination der Fiskalpolitik: Wohlfahrtsökonomische versus Politökonomische Sicht" in *Jahrbuch für Wirtschaftswissenschaften* [Review of Economics] 48, 1997, pp. 174–92.

Clemens Fuest, "Der dritte Systemwettbewerb" in *Frankfurter Allgemeine Zeitung*, July 27, 2018, p. 18.

Clemens Fuest, Nils Goldschmidt, Bernd Lucke, Birger P. Priddat, and Gert G. Wagner, "Abkehr von der Ordnungspolitik in der Ökonomie?" *Wirtschaftsdienst*, 86 (1), 2006, pp. 7–25.

Nils Goldschmidt and Stefan Kolev, *75 Jahre Soziale Marktwirtschaft* (Freiburg in Breisgau: Herder, 2023).

Paul Kirchhof, "Recht gibt es nicht zum Niedrigpreis" in *Frankfurter Allgemeine Zeitung*, December 1, 2004, p. 38.

Alfred Müller-Armack, *Wirtschaftslenkung und Marktwirtschaft*, special edn. (Munich: Kastell Verlag, 1946/1990).

Alfred Müller-Armack, "Das gesellschaftspolitische Leitbild der Sozialen Marktwirtschaft" in Alfred Müller-Armack, *Wirtschaftsordnung und Wirtschaftspolitik, Studien und Konzepte zur Sozialen Marktwirtschaft und zur Europäischen Integration* (Freiburg in Breisgau: Verlag Rombach, 1960/1966), pp. 293–315.

Alfred Müller-Armack, "Die zweite Phase der Sozialen Marktwirtschaft" in Alfred Müller-Armack, *Wirtschaftsordnung und Wirtschaftspolitik, Studien und Konzepte zur Sozialen Marktwirtschaft und zur Europäischen Integration* (Freiburg in Breisgau: Verlag Rombach, 1962/66), pp. 267–91.

Alfred Müller-Armack, "The Social Market Economy as an Economic and Social Order" in *Review of Social Economy*, 36:3 (1978), pp. 325–31.

Wilhelm Röpke, *Die Gesellschaftskrisis der Gegenwart* (Erlenbach-Zürich: Eugen Rentsch Verlag, 1942/1948).

Wilhelm Röpke, *Maß und Mitte* (Erlenbach-Zürich: Eugen Rentsch Verlag, 1950).

Wilhelm Röpke, *Jenseits von Angebot und Nachfrage* (Repr. Düsseldorf: Verlagsanstalt Handwerk, 1958).

Hans-Werner Sinn, "Der neue Systemwettbewerb" in *Perspektiven der Wirtschaftspolitik* 3 (2002), pp. 391–407.

Charles M. Tiebout, "A Pure Theory of Local Expenditures" in *Journal of Political Economy* 64, (1956), pp. 416–24.

Viktor Vanberg, "Auch Staaten tut Wettbewerb gut: Eine Replik auf Paul Kirchhof" in *Freiburger Diskussionspapiere zur Ordnungsökonomik*, no. 05/2, Albert-Ludwigs-Universität Freiburg, Institut für Allgemeine Wirtschaftsforschung, Abteilung für Wirtschaftspolitik (Freiburg in Breisgau, 2005).

George Zodrow and Peter Mieszkowski, "Pigou, Tiebout, Property Taxation, and the Underprovision of Local Public Goods" in *Journal of Urban Economics* 19 (1986), pp. 356–70.

CHAPTER 7

THE IMMUTABLE BRAIN?
AND YET IT MOVES!

MARTIN KORTE

The real crisis of our times [...] is not that we don't have it good, or even that we might be worse off later on. No, the real crisis is that we can't come up with anything better.

Rutger Bregman, *Utopia for Realists*, 2017

"How can we create a free, just, and sustainable world?" is a question that is just as fundamental as the Ecce Homo question and, as such, it is an important distinction to superficial thinking: Such questions prevent thinking from being too short-sighted or going round in circles, and also prevent the situation

143

that William James described as follows: "A great many people think they are thinking when they are merely rearranging their prejudices."

At the moment, the real question is how a free, just, and sustainable world can be preserved while maintaining biodiversity and slowing global warming. Life is always in flux, as is our world. So the topic of "preservation" is not about freezing a situation, but rather maintaining free, just, and sustainable systems homeostatically within certain parameters.

Weather is a daily experience, while climate is an abstract statistical mean of average temperatures, precipitation, and wind speeds. Biodiversity is a no less abstract concept that goes far beyond observing different species of birds on the pond or bird feeder in your own garden. And that's where the problems for our brains begin. What we cannot understand in the truest sense of the word, what is not immediately observable, always escapes our attention and thus our scope for action.

Sociologists, lawyers, and economists look at the systemic conditions that control and regulate societies or monetary value systems and that both create and define the scope for action. Of course, people also play a role here, but in the context of higher systemic boundaries. This is, of course, valuable. But particularly when it comes to preserving natural diversity or slowing down climate change, an examination of our (individual) brain may be just as helpful, because this is the organ with which politicians have to work in the short and long term, as do voters, company bosses, and employees. It is therefore this organ above all others that, on an individual level, creates resistance to changes in perception, thinking, and ultimately action, or enables change through learning processes, or, on the political, economic or legal stage, is involved in the possibly incorrect definition of systemic conditions.

"THE BRAIN IS WIDER THAN THE SKY" (EMILY DICKINSON)

We do not perceive the world clearly, but rather in the way the preset, partly learned, partly genetic wiring in our brain presents it to us. Free will is also tricky. We humans are not very aware of what we are perceiving, nor are we aware of what we think, or even why we perform certain actions—we are more like observers of our decisions than the directors of the movie of our lives and experiences. The brain actually conceals a lot from our imaginary self, without wanting to suggest through this choice of words that the self and the brain are different entities, nor that we know exactly what this self is, at least from the neuroscience perspective.

All of these preliminary remarks are an introduction to the fact that thinking about human decision-making processes, whether in the political or private sphere, involves a series of heuristic, often unconscious preconceptions—also referred to as distortions (bias)—which, however, already subject these preconceptions to evaluation. From an evolutionary perspective, one might argue that the brain often has to make quick, vitally important decisions in a complex environment that's presenting ambiguous signals, and that, given the lack of data, it has to rely on these preconceptions (i.e. on our intuitions, whose primary value has been repeatedly emphasized by the psychologist Gerd Gigerenzer).[1] In the era of hunter-gatherers, our ancestor who contemplated and reflected on the fact that the pawing noises going on behind him reminded him of pleasant sounds in another context probably didn't survive to be our ancestor—unlike the one who quickly jumped out of the way.

So, in lots of decision-making situations the brain employs processes that—at least if one does not switch on slow, reflective, frontal-lobe-based thinking—make use of "mental shortcuts." All of this can be adaptive, but in times of disruption, intuitions whose "knowledge" relates to what is known, familiar, and already experienced, are poor advisors. This may also apply to our present times, and so intuitions and "felt truths" become problems, especially when it comes to processes of adapting to climate change, nature conservation, or issues of biodiversity.

One of these disruptive distortions (biases) in the working processes of our brain (when conditions are changing rapidly) is to persist with what we have started, even when things are clearly going badly, on the stock market or in other projects, for example. We are afraid of losing and have too little faith in the chances a change of course might bring. When it comes to climate issues, too, we shy away from looking open-mindedly at alternative behaviors and the real pressure to change our policy. We also tend to prefer simple explanations to complicated ones, but paradoxically at the same time we tend to look for unnecessarily complicated solutions rather than simple ones. Solving problems by leaving something out is not part of the brain's natural way of finding a solution.

Our brains have other habits that can have problematic effects when it comes to shaping the future. For example, when we find food sources, our brains tend to take in more calories than we use (if we have the opportunity, since the brain itself does not store energy, it needs an external reservoir which is found in abdominal fat).[2] Brains have a preset, inherent desire to generally "want more," whether it's happiness, more than our neighbor, or more than we had yesterday. This has always driven people to explore, invent, or achieve new things, but it also leads to a waste of resources.

It is also extremely damaging for long-term adaptation processes, which also generate costs to mental health, that we find it hard to see our future self as our own self. Imaging techniques show that when we think about ourselves in the future, the same areas of the brain become active that are also activated when we think about strangers. It is therefore hard to project the negative consequences of actions today onto a self who is a "stranger."

If life circumstances change, we should change too. It is therefore all the more worrying that we tend to block out perceptions that do not match our expectations. Our brain constantly makes assumptions about the future (called "predictive coding") and views even the present as part of a paradoxical arrow of time that illuminates the present from the expected future, seeking first of all confirmation of these predictions, which can all too often be deceptive. This mental shortcut often prejudices the way we think and perceive, and is also known as "confirmation bias."

This describes the fact that we find it difficult, even at the perceptual level, to recognize facts and situations that do not correspond to our previous environmental experience and thus our preconceived opinion. Thus, quick first impressions become the permanent basis for decisions, which can lead to preconceptions and incorrect judgments without us noticing, even when we believe we have done everything right ("... the worst is well-intentioned").

The brain's underlying processing principle is that it tries to anticipate what will happen next at every moment of our lives in order to adapt both the sensory system and our thoughts and actions to a future situation (even if it is seconds in advance) in order to then minimize the "prediction error" as much as possible (this alone is experienced as a reward). This prediction error can and should of course be minimized through adaptation and learning, but unfortunately it is more convenient to look for confirmation of what we expected.[3]

Another important aspect in this context is that our potential ability to understand and respond effectively to environmental risks is also negatively impacted by the way we respond to threats and losses. We prioritize those risks that we perceive as certain, that are happening here and now, and that affect ourselves and the people who are important to us. Unfortunately, for many people climate change still seems like a threat that is far away in space and time, and the extent and nature of its impact on them personally remain unclear—this effect is even more evident in the case of biodiversity.

It is therefore a major challenge to focus on climate change and other environmental risks in order to motivate both individuals and communities to act. Accordingly, environmental educators and communications experts have long struggled with the issue of how best to motivate people to engage with climate change and the necessary changes in our daily behavior that it entails. The debate is about the extent to which narratives of hope or narratives of fear are best suited to promoting environmentally friendly action. Negative information is more likely to be ignored in decision-making, which increases the likelihood that "gloomy" scenarios regarding climate change will not be taken into account.

In all of this, experts should consider what the French sociologist Pierre Bourdieu identified under the term "scholastic fallacy." This is the tendency of scientists to assume that all people think about problems in the same way as this very special group of people. Bourdieu thus warns against experts in public discourse distorting reality when they overlook the fact that most people cannot devote the time and effort to thinking about these questions in the same way as those for whom this is a full-time job. Academics often fail to recognize this and are baffled when the public does not understand that interpretations are constantly being revised in the light of new data, as has happened almost constantly throughout scientific history, since such revisions are necessary to change our conception of how the world, our bodies, or our very ways of thinking works. The data available to the public is also less dependent on statistical tests than on the language of communication and graphic imagery, and very often the authenticity of the scientist and their communication skills are even more important than data, facts, and figures. To paraphrase a quote by Bill Clinton, one would like to emphasize to all scientists: "It's the person, stupid!"

UNCERTAINTY AND AMBIGUITY

There are known knowns ... But there are also unknown unknowns.

Former US Secretary of State for Defense, Donald Rumsfeld, at a 2002 press conference.

Now, much is known about why our brains are quick to pursue short-term rewards and have difficulty giving these up in order to pursue long-term goals such as preserving biodiversity and slowing climate change. We also know a lot about why our brains have such a hard time changing habits: It simply saves on the energy used for thinking when we don't have to constantly think about our actions and deeds but act automatically to avoid the actual work of thinking, as Thomas Edison put it over a hundred years ago. Unfortunately, humans find it very hard to adjust to the uncertainties of a future world of climate change, and it is particularly worrying that humans can more easily deal with known risks, i.e. with uncertainties. Here it is worth taking a look into the engine room of the brain to determine how we keep running aground while navigating the data jungle. This is also because different areas of the brain are involved. For example, uncertainty activates the amygdala (which produces fear and with it a feeling of negativity) and the anterior cingulate cortex, which is located inside the cerebral cortex between the two cerebral hemispheres, and which conveys another negative feeling, namely the presence of conflicts. On the other hand, there is the striatum, part of the basal ganglia in the brain, which is primarily involved in risk calculation, and at the same time corresponds with the brain's reward centers. In short, from the brain's point of view, uncertainty conveys fear and potential conflicts, while risk calculation also offers the prospect of rewards.

Here's an example of how we react to uncertainty and risk in our decisions. Imagine you have two urns in front of you. Each urn contains 100 balls. You are given a clear description of the contents of the first urn: 50 red balls and 50 black balls. The scientist conducting the experiment says nothing about the second urn and only says that the 100 balls are divided between red and black in a certain ratio. You are then given a choice. Say you're offered a bet on drawing a red ball from one of the two urns: if your choice is correct, you will receive a certain amount of money if you actually draw a red ball. Which urn would you like to draw from? You then have a second attempt, but you are asked to choose a black ball. Which urn will you choose this time?

A clear majority of the subjects choose the first urn both times, even though this choice means that there could be more or fewer red balls than in the second urn. This result—uncertainty versus risk—is known as the Ellsberg Paradox, named for Daniel Ellsberg, who called this behavior "ambiguity aversion" (a kind of mental allergy to uncertainty). This provides evidence that knowing the exact probability of circumstances can greatly influence and alter decision-making.

The experiment thus reveals a deeper problem whereby our brains, with their aversion to uncertainty, stand in the way of long-term problem-solving, such as tackling climate change. Not only are the probabilities of the outcomes unknown—for example, the real probability of hurricanes in the Caribbean in ten years' time—but also the damage they might cause (even if climate change caused by humans is itself a fact, there are indeed lots of uncertainties).

But this too can be made more concrete and thus more tangible, in the hope that the specific amount that will soon have to be paid, for example in relation to home insurance, will be quantifiable. Indeed, ignorance of the future already has a monetary value in insurance terms: uncertainty makes risks expensive to insure and often even unaffordable. The less insurance companies know about the risks, the more capital they need to protect their balance sheets against possible losses. In May 2024 State Farm, California's largest home insurer, withdrew from the market entirely, arguing that the cost of "rapidly growing disaster risk" was too high.

However, there is one important difference between the urn example given above and climate change: climate models are based on physical laws that can be studied. It is as if a climate scientist has been observing the second urn for centuries and noting the number of black and red balls drawn by different people over time. With solid evidence and a clear understanding of the process by which the observations were produced, the uncertainty disappears, and the probabilities of potential disasters are better understood.

But even a perfect scientific model could not remove all uncertainties. Climate change is as much about the chaotic world of politics as it is about the clarity of physics. Scientists may be able to model how a planet that is 2°C warmer than in pre-industrial times increases the risk of wildfires in a particular area. But there is no model that can predict whether policy-makers will use the levers at their disposal to prevent such fires. However, we can control how we ourselves act, each of us on a small scale, but overall also on a larger scale, to influence which political framework we are willing to accept in order to bequeath a habit-able world to our children.

HEAT AND HEAT-SENSITIVE BRAINS

In order to change behavior in relation to impending climate change and how it can be mitigated as much as possible, the consequences for humans must perhaps be made even clearer. After all, climate change affects not only coral reefs and people who live near water but each and every one of us through the increase in heavy rain events, storms, long periods of drought and, last but not least, the occurrence of heatwaves.[4]

For the brain to do its job, various conditions must be met. Brain development must follow certain genetic pathways; it must be supplied with nutrients and operate within a narrow range of physical parameters such as temperature; it must receive input and generate output. If these conditions are not met, brain function can be impaired, for example by hypoxia, poisoning (alcohol, drugs), sleep disorders, psychological trauma, and other illnesses. Extremes in temperature can also exceed the brain's ability to compensate more quickly than one might think.[5] Brain function that is impaired as a result of a heatwave can negatively impact the person's ability to respond to external challenges. Resilience can be impaired in an acute or chronic way. People with brain disorders are less able to cope with change.[6]

Acutely impaired brain function has proven consequences and costs. By contrast, acute, large-scale environmental stresses that have direct consequences for brain function are less directly tangible for humans. This is the case with heatwaves. Surprisingly, only a few studies exist on the consequences of heatwaves specifically for brain function, but it is clear that they have disastrous effects on health, especially in less resilient people. Homeothermic human beings have a thermoregulation system, some aspects of which have been externalized, for example clothing, heating, exercise, and housing. But both internal and external thermoregulation have their limits. Given a sufficiently unfavorable combination of circumstances, people still freeze to death during cold snaps or die during heatwaves. For example, the 2003 heatwave in Europe resulted in over 20,000 heat-related deaths, and all current climate models assume that heatwaves will increase in number and increasingly reach record temperatures. Above 41°C, heat becomes life-threatening, especially for people with health problems, and for the elderly just as much as for small children.

It is a complex task to provide the brain with the working environment it needs. During a heatwave, people need to know that the ambient temperature is forcing them to act and they need to be able to react accordingly. If it is too hot, they may need to move to a cooler place, seek shade, drink more, take off clothing, open windows, change the settings on their environmental systems, and refrain from exertion. Intrinsic thermoregulatory responses, such as sweating, must work. If these responses fail, the temperature of the brain and its host body can rise to levels that further impair brain function and can eventually lead to heat-related death, in which brain dysfunction plays a central role.

When the functioning of the brain itself is impaired, its ability to respond to environmental demands can decline.

Climate change is happening. Even if human-generated greenhouse gas emissions ceased tomorrow, further increases in global temperatures remain inevitable due to the long-lived greenhouse gases already present in the atmosphere. The all-pervasive concerns surrounding global warming are becoming clearer every day as more research is done. Climate change will lead to more frequent and more intensive environmental problems. Heatwaves alone are becoming more severe and more frequent. The pace and extent of damage to the world's climate caused by humans has implications for all living things.

Many people have recently had to find out that it's hard to work during a heatwave. People with neurological (and other) conditions are likely to be affected first. Heat limits the brain's performance, makes us more aggressive, and can lead to death in the event of extreme overheating—the brain is more sensitive to heat than any other organ in the human body.

SUSTAINABILITY PRESUPPOSES A CHANGE
IN THE BRAIN

> There are these two young fish swimming along. And
> they happen to meet an older fish swimming the other
> way. Who nods at them and says "Morning, boys.
> How's the water?" And the two young fish swim on
> for a bit. And then eventually one of them looks over
> at the other and goes "What the hell is water?"
>
> David Foster Wallace[7]

Don't worry—in the last section of this essay I'm
not going as some "wise old fish." Instead, I'd like to
explore the question of why habits make it so hard to
adapt our behavior as well as to be more flexible in our
thinking.

Habits are good when we can quickly and reliably
get back into our work routine after a long break, or
still know how to drive a car. But our brain cannot
distinguish between good habits and bad habits,
which causes problems, especially when it comes to
altering behavior in light of climate change. Most
people believe that their behavior is motivated by
certain intentions. However, according to psychological studies this only applies to activities that have
not yet become automatic. The more often they are
repeated, the more the original goal fades and the

159

context becomes more important—we do things in certain places, at certain times, and in certain constellations without thinking about it in the moment. Areas of the basal ganglia below the cerebral cortex that are not involved in language are primarily involved in the formation of habits, and the activity of these areas of the brain usually does not reach our consciousness.

So can habits be changed when we understand the positive effects of less stress or sustainable and healthy eating? Scientists have examined whether personal goals and behaviors can be changed through targeted programs. The result was that although the programs changed the subjects' intentions, and they ultimately believed deeply and firmly in their new goals of more healthy eating or more sustainable behavior, this nevertheless had little impact on their eating habits and behaviors that would have a lasting effect on their carbon footprint.

Therefore, there seems little point in focusing on long-term goals alone if we want to change the old habits of individuals, and especially of an entire culture. Appeals and expressions of goodwill do not lead to lasting changes in behavior!

To do this, programs that try to change habits collectively in a social group are more promising. So, as a whole family, you can resolve to eat more healthily, or as a team to reduce the amount of waste produced at work, or to cycle to work instead of driving. It also helps to imagine the new situation in every detail. If you want to minimize stress, you have to visualize what everyday life would look like, what you have to change, and what you want to do differently, and then the chances of implementing this are greater, and not everyone in the group has to think about every decision each time. It also helps to think about the stimuli that trigger a behavior. (It is much easier to order online with the result that consumption, and thus carbon footprint, increase quickly. When shopping, sustainability takes a back seat. So whenever you find something interesting, sleep on it, and think about whether you can buy the product locally—if you still want it the next day.)

It takes eighteen to twenty-one days to develop a habit—and usually twice as long to get rid of it again, and you can only do that if you replace an old routine with a new one. So it is, and remains, hard to change habits of perception, thought, and action, especially when it comes to habits of perception, thought, and action that have been practiced for many years and sometimes over decades as part of a cultural, social, or economic system.

However, habits and routines are not just troublesome stumbling blocks to our real desires. They are quantitatively the most common cause of our actions; if you want to change them, you have to take them very seriously. It has been shown that it is not enough to just re-adjust one's goals, but that above all old habits have to be replaced by new ones. Habits, just like culturally established processes, consist of many unconscious and automatic decisions that we make every day. Just by looking out for them, they become visible again—which, incidentally, also changes our political view of the world, because in the end the only thing that counts in a measurable way is what entire countries can change. Only when maladaptive (environmental) habits become visible can we try to control them and slowly but surely change them—defeats are inevitable here and no reason to give up altogether.

A meta-analysis of fifty studies[8] also shows how difficult it is for an individual to change. Through concrete interventions in various experiments, scientists have tried to change the personal goals and behavior of test subjects. Seen overall the result of all these studies was devastating. The scientists managed to convince the test subjects of their new goals, but after a short time their behavior fell back into old patterns. It therefore seems pointless to orient your behavior idealistically towards sustainability if you want to break old habits.

However, when the controlled interventions with test subjects were designed not only to bring about recognition of the need for a change in behavior, but also to practice very specific new routines and habits, the success rate was much higher. Above all, these studies showed that people are most likely to change their routines when the changes are not forced upon them, but rather when they adopt them of their own free will. In addition, they found it easier to change routines when they were part of a social group. And it also helped them to simulate the goal to be achieved as precisely as possible, even to imagine it in every detail. If you can also make the new routine seem familiar and use new triggers, the threshold for learning a new routine (and forgetting a bad habit more quickly) is lower. Even more amazingly, you can actually strengthen your willpower to change a habit by exercising it, which is subordinate to the executive function of the frontal lobe, and which is constantly weakened when you're multitasking on your cellphone, but strengthened when you're engaging in sport, playing music, or reading a book.

"At critical moments in time," writes Tyler Cowen in his blog *Marginal Revolution*, "you can raise the aspirations of other people significantly, especially when they are relatively young, simply by suggesting they do something better or more ambitious than what they might have in mind. It costs you relatively little to do this, but the benefit to them, and to the broader world, may be enormous. This is in fact one of the most valuable things you can do with your time and with your life."[9]

Notes

1. Gerd Gigerenzer, *The Intelligence of Intuition* (Cambridge: CUP, 2023).

2. Daniel Lieberman, *Exercised: The Science of Physical Activity, Rest and Health* (London: Penguin, 2021).

3. See the wonderful discussion in Andy Clark, *The Experience Machine: How Our Minds Predict and Shape Reality* (London: Penguin, 2024).

4. Cf. also WHO, "Results Report: Program Budget 2022–2023." https://www.who.int/about/accountability/results/who-results-report-2022-2023 (accessed December 17, 2024).

5. Clayton P. Aldern, *The Weight of Nature: How a Changing Climate Changes Our Minds, Brains, and Bodies* (London: Penguin, 2024); Jeff Goodell, *The Heat Will Kill You First: Life and Death on a Scorched Planet* (New York: Little, Brown, 2023).

6. See also Li Lan, Jieyu Tang, Pavel Wargocki, David P. Wyon, Zihiwei Lian, "Cognitive performance was reduced

by higher air temperature even when thermal comfort was maintained over the 24–28°C range" in *Indoor Air* 32:e12916 (2022). https://doi.org/10.1111/ina.12916 (accessed December 3, 2024).

7. David Foster Wallace, "Parable of the Fish" from the commencement speech to the graduating class at Kenyon College (2005).

8. Summarized in Charles Duhigg, *The Power of Habit: Why We Do What We Do, and How to Change* (New York: Random House, 2013).

9. Tyler Cowen, "The high-return activity of raising others' aspirations" in *Marginal Revolution*, October 21, 2018. https://marginalrevolution.com/marginalrevolution/2018/10/high-return-activity-raising-others-aspirations.html (accessed January 28, 2025).

Further Reading

Jared Diamond, *Collapse: How Societies Choose to Fail or Survive* (London: Penguin, 2011).

Henning Beck, *12 Gesetze der Dummheit: Denkfehler, die vernünftige Entscheidungen in der Politik und bei uns allen verhindern* (Berlin: Econ Verlag, 2023).

Gerhard Roth, *Warum es so schwierig ist, sich und andere zu ändern: Persönlichkeit, Entscheidung und Verhalten* (Stuttgart: Klett-Cotta, 2019).

CHAPTER 8

UNDERSTANDING, VOLUNTARY PARTICIPATION, PERSUASION, ENFORCEMENT—REGULATION AS A STEP TOWARDS A FREE, JUST, AND SUSTAINABLE WORLD

STEFAN KORIOTH

I.

In his second published *Sketchbook* [diary], Max Frisch expressed his fundamental skepticism about people's ability to change for the better via non-authoritarian means and their ability to hope for this: "In regard to the world situation, do you hope: a. that reason will prevail? b. that a miracle will occur? c. that everything will go on as before?" And: "If you had the power to implement what you feel to be right, would you implement it against the will of the majority? Yes or no."[1] Everyone knows that today, fifty years later, in view of the threat posed by climate change to the survival of life on Earth, every individual and humanity as a whole must find different and—in the wealthy countries—less agreeable lifestyles and habits, and as fast as possible. This is true regardless of whether climate change can still be stopped or whether we already have to focus on minimizing the consequences.[2] A global population of almost eight billion people is pushing the planet to its limits; growth linked to energy consumption is exceeding the Earth's productive capacities and threatening global society. Carbon dioxide produced by fossil fuels remains in the atmosphere and is heating up the Earth. "This means that the Earth's temperature will continue to rise as long as we burn oil, gas, and coal. If we want to stabilize the temperature, we have to reduce this rise to zero."[3]

But how is this supposed to happen, how is what is described in a somewhat detached way by the rather meaningless word "transformation" supposed to succeed? This is also a question for smart regulation that has clear goals and evaluates possible measures.

How a society is structured, what it regards as desirable or undesirable behavior, and which procedures and decisions it uses to distinguish one from the other, is expressed through its rules and norms, today usually through its legal system. The following essay is less about the content of such rules for transformation, and more about how convenience, habits, and self-interest can be overcome or used in order to attain the goal of transformation.

II.

As an example—one of many emotionally charged ones—let us take the regulation of freight transportation and private transport on the roads, a significant and, in terms of qualitative extent, persistent source of environmentally harmful emissions. Does it make sense in the near future to ban the use of internal combustion (IC) engines powered by fossil fuels? Or, instead of a ban, are there less rigid forms of regulation that guarantee just as much or more success in preventing emissions?

Psychological and anthropological conditions and obstacles that affect the context of such regulation are to a large extent understood and rarely disputed. Change we must—the ability to understand and the options for decision-making and action exist. Nevertheless, change is hard. The neuroscientist Gerhard Roth points out that basic personality traits are established early on and are difficult to change. Whether a person is dynamic and open or cautious and stubborn, optimistic or pessimistic, are some of the almost immutable basic facts pertaining to every individual. To change behavior, Roth recommends identifying clear goals, familiarization, developing routines, and (self-administered) rewards both large and small.[4] They can be used to counteract opposing forces that include the tendency towards instant gratification rather than working towards long-term goals, laziness and complacency, overestimating short-term consequences and underestimating the long-term consequences of behavior (present bias), and vacillating between egoism and altruism.

This forms the basis for tried and tested tools that can control behavior, but not attitudes. They are primarily requirements and prohibitions—moral, legal, and criminal—and various forms of indirect behavior control through incentives, by pointing out attractive or less attractive options. Moreover, the existing state of road transport in Germany, as it relates to climate, is well-known:

In Germany, around 20% of greenhouse-gas [GHG] emissions are generated in the transport sector [...] Between 1990 and 2023, GHG emissions in Germany overall fell by 46% [...]. Emissions in the transport sector, by contrast, have remained almost constant. The proportion of total emissions caused by transport has thus increased from around 13% in 1990 to 21.6% in 2023. The COVID-19 pandemic led to merely a short-term decline in GHG emissions in the transport sector. One third of the GHG emissions in the transport sector and the resulting negative impact on climate are caused by freight transportation. Commercial vehicles as a proportion of total transport emissions has increased in recent years.[5]

This problem is reflected in the effects of Germany's Climate Change Act. According to Annex 2 to Section 4 of the Climate Change Act, a maximum of 145 million tonnes of CO_2 should have been generated in the transport sector in 2021, but in fact—and despite COVID-19—it was 148 million tonnes.

Against this backdrop, the European Union has decided to implement drastic measures without protracted preparations. From 2035, only new vehicles without an IC engine will be permitted for sale. Old vehicles may still be used and traded. However, given the massive resistance in some sectors, it seems unclear whether this ban will actually remain in this form. At present—fall 2024—there is a heated debate about whether the ban should be maintained. The President of the European Commission has instructed Commissioner Hoekstra, who is responsible for climate protection, to "put the 2035 IC engine ban to the test." Independently of this, for a long time the EU has been implementing (fleet) emission limits on new cars, which should reduce to 94 g/km from 2025. This too is suddenly up for discussion—again in fall 2024. Car manufacturers are calling for the new limits to be postponed, particularly in view of the critical state of the automobile industry in the EU.[6] The legal basis for this, it is argued, is Article 122 of the Treaty on the Functioning of the European Union (TFEU), which allows the Commission to take action in economic emergencies.

It is remarkable that to control behavior the EU has resorted to the most stringent of possible instruments— except for criminal law. A ban does not prompt any alternative forms of behavior. It contains a clear statement that consumers and vehicle manufacturers can adapt to—with greater or lesser difficulties. At the same time, there are concerns. Is the measure, in particular the reference to e-mobility, really aimed at replacing resource-consuming options with resource-saving options? In the context of the IC engine ban, it became known that the comparison between damage to the climate caused by IC engines and that caused electric cars was being made literally at the level of the exhaust pipe. Clearly, the environmental impact of providing electrical energy was completely ignored. While this can easily be changed, other concerns are not easy to dispel. Banning a certain kind of technology is explicitly anti-technology and anti-business. Such a harsh instrument may only be used if there are extremely important reasons for doing so, particularly if less drastic ways of reducing emissions cannot be attempted, such as an absolute cap on CO_2 emissions or carbon pricing. Moreover, focusing on a particular technology in the EU ignores what is happening, permitted, or desired in other parts of the world. Ultimately, the ban is very demanding in practical terms if mobility is to be maintained. What about electricity production and charging infrastructure? Might a ban on IC engine technology cause undesirable social upheaval because the new technology, with its associated high prices, creates significant barriers to access?

III.

A ban is simple and clear, but what comes next may not be that simple after all. The short and still ongoing history of the IC engine ban thus far not only reflects the attempt to send a clear signal. It also shows that it is disastrous to discuss and take issue with the ban again after it has been clearly imposed. If the ban's subjects do not know what rules are to apply, or must assume that everything could be different tomorrow, the persuasiveness of the ban is lost. In such a case, the measure is subject to debate without regard to its objectives. Shortly after the ban was questioned, it was claimed that two thirds of the German population rejected an IC engine ban, but that "those who control the cultural means of production and therefore set the agenda are no longer concerned."[7] Such statements are no longer about climate protection, about the choice of technologies and options for action, but instead they are asserting the usual forces of inertia against change. Of course, the appeal to a majority carries weight. But how can anyone be certain that a two-thirds majority—indeed, such a majority as is required to amend the Constitution—actually does not want to change anything?

Such objections to a ban on IC engines show that other strategies are advisable and must be drawn up. In the EU and Member States' range of approaches, bans have long been making way for other instruments that are mainly based on cooperation. The sudden, harsh implementation of a ban on IC engines, albeit with a preparation and adjustment phase until 2035, shows that reverting to this approach provokes resistance that is not conducive to the aim on which there is widespread agreement. Affordable personal mobility is indispensable for many, necessary (for commuters in rural areas), or simply an expression of freedom. In Germany some people went so far as to assert a "fundamental right to mobility" using one's own car, which, however, was not granted—and rightly so.[8] Conversely, the individual equally has the right to claim that the municipality or state should guarantee a certain level of public transport services, especially in the form of local and long-distance passenger transport. The need to transport freight by road is indispensable for the economy for the foreseeable future: rail, air, and (inland) shipping alternatives are reaching their infrastructural limits, as is the lack of availability of transport options, including rail connections and accessibility to ports, and finally the speed of transport.

In this context, an attempt should be made to try a "technology-neutral approach" (as EU Commission President Ursula von der Leyen put it) with incentives to implement particular climate protection solutions. This means a combination of instruments that could begin by making CO_2 emissions even more expensive than before, thereby making the use of IC engines less attractive.[9] But this in turn has its limits. National carbon pricing and other costs (with regard to EU law or vehicle tolls) are already making the operation of (diesel) trucks in particular increasingly expensive. Recently, however, road transport systems have proven to be surprisingly price-insensitive. This will remain the case as long as the conditions for using alternative vehicle technologies do not change, ranging from adequate charging infrastructure and affordable electricity prices to a functioning secondary market for electric vehicles. Moreover, it is debatable whether subsidies are a suitable and economical instrument for changing behavior. On the one hand, it has been shown that buyers' premiums for purchasing electric cars have had a huge impact: when they were significantly reduced in Germany, sales of previously subsidized vehicles collapsed drastically. On the other hand, subsidies are so costly that in practice both the EU and Germany can only pay for them by taking on new debt.

IV.

Behavioral changes in the face of unavoidable and even existential challenges that affect everyone, not just the individual: In such cases only a combination of guidance, persuasion, incentives, and bans can help. But above all, a kind of partnership must be established between law-makers and their target groups, and the useful and acceptable aspects of new behaviors ("framing") must be highlighted. This is how we can set the limits that are necessary for the future of our societies. "Setting limits preserves the freedom of us all."[10] Instead of primarily debating instruments, rule-making that is based on freedom can help. It would have to take into account the principle that has long been practiced in law, particularly in risk prevention law and environmental law: the "polluter pays" principle.

Every state, every institution, every individual must be held accountable for their own actions that damage the climate—and must come up with alternatives. Those who cause climate damage should pay for the elimination of such damage or compensate for it. Democratic and market-based structures are the most compatible with a consistent implementation of this principle, at least if it includes social compensation measures which, in an ecological democracy, are as necessary as the mechanisms of the market economy being complemented by the welfare state.

Notes

1. Max Frisch, *Sketchbook 1966–1971*, trans. Simon Pare (London: Seagull Books, 2023).

2. A committed statement on this can be found in Jonathan Franzen, *What If We Stopped Pretending?* (London: Fourth Estate, 2021).

3. Anders Levermann, "Kein Reichtum ohne Gesellschaft" in *FAZ*, September 23, 2024, p. 11.

4. Gerhard Roth, *Warum es so schwierig ist, sich und andere zu ändern* (Stuttgart: Klett-Cotta Verlag, 2021).

5. German Council of Economic Experts, spring report, May 15, 2024, p. 83.

6. On both, see "Rebellion gegen Milliardenstrafen" in *FAZ*, September 20, 2024, p. 17.

7. Kristina Schröder, "Die kulturelle Hegemonie derjenigen, die Klimaschutz jeglicher Abwägung enthoben betrachten" in *Die Welt*, July 31, 2024, www.welt.de/debatte/kommentare/plus252630002/Verbrennerverbot-Wie-die-Oeko-Bewegung-die-Lebensrealitaet-vieler-Deutscher-negiert.html (accessed November 18, 2024).

8. For the argument in favor, see Michael Ronellenfitsch, "Die Verkehrsmobilität als Grund- und Menschenrecht" in *Jahrbuch für öffentliches Recht* 44 (1996), pp. 167–203; Ronellenfitsch, "Mobilität: Vom Grundbedürfnis zum Grundrecht?" *Deutsches Auto-Recht* (1992), pp. 321–25.

9. See Ottmar Edenhofer and Corinne Flick, "Warum am CO2-Preis kein Weg vorbeiführt" Convoco! Podcast (113), March 2024. https://www.convoco.co.uk/podcast/113-ottmar-edenhofer-warum-am-co2-preis-kein-weg-vorbei-fuehrt/ (accessed November 18, 2024).

10. See Levermann, "Kein Reichtum ohne Gesellschaft."

CHAPTER 9

REGULATION FOR A FREE, JUST, AND SUSTAINABLE DIGITAL FUTURE

BIRKE HÄCKER

I. BRAVE NEW DIGITAL WORLD

Rarely—if ever in the history of humankind—has the technical environment of a society changed so drastically in so brief a time as over the past half century. In the long-term perspective, it is but the blink of an eye since the first personal computers entered our private and professional lives during the 1980s. A rapid series of further developments followed in ever shorter intervals: from the emergence of the internet in the 1990s, via the rise of social media and the ubiquitous spread of smartphones, to cloud computing, blockchain technology, and the latest advances in artificial intelligence (AI). We have truly experienced a digital transformation; in an allusion to the industrial revolution of the 19th century, some even speak of a "digital revolution".[1] Nowadays, politicians govern via social media almost on a routine basis, and US presidents first announce their withdrawal from the race for re-election on X (formerly Twitter); in our homes, there are remote-controlled smart devices connected to each other and to the outside world via the "internet of things"; and even works of art can be bought in purely virtual form, as non-fungible tokens, so-called NFTs. In short, the "digital age" has not merely begun—for many people it already determines large parts of their everyday lives, particularly in Europe and other regions of the so-called Global North.

This development presents our society with numerous and diverse new challenges. Digital technologies make life more interesting and more convenient, yet they also make us more vulnerable. Just think of the spread of fake news and hate speech on the internet; the emergence of social bubbles and echo chambers that distort normal social discourse and may even undermine it surreptitiously; or think of the danger that a cyberattack or simply a failed security update can cripple infrastructure on a global scale, as happened with the CrowdStrike incident in July 2024. On the one hand, the emerging digital world offers new scope for personal development, it helps create and maintain social contact over long distances, and it provides numerous opportunities for participating in political processes. On the other hand, however, this brave new digital world itself poses real risks for individual freedom and equality, for human interaction, and ultimately for the very foundations of democracy. In the minds of many, the perception of danger culminated when in 2023 a group of leading figures from the world's premier technology companies and specialists in relevant disciplines issued a public warning through the media about the risks inherent in artificial intelligence (AI), saying that if left unfettered, AI has the long-term potential to decimate or even wipe out humankind.[2]

II. INSTRUMENTS FOR REGULATING DIGITAL CHALLENGES

In light of the situation outlined above, it is important to consider whether and how these new digital technologies can and should be regulated. By "regulation" is meant (in the broadest possible sense) the imposition of certain rules, standards and frameworks, either by the state or supranationally, within which the technologies must evolve and be applied. The fundamental need for such regulation has been obvious for a long time. It is merely on the questions of how intensive this regulation should be, and whether it should be primarily preventive (*ex ante* regulation) or retrospective, through a liability regime sounding in damages when things go wrong (*ex post* regulation), that opinions differ.

In abstract terms, there is always a trade-off: the more intensive the regulation of new technologies within a particular market, the greater the inevitable concomitant inhibition of innovation, reducing the international competitiveness of companies active in this market. Yet the less regulation there is, the more likely the risks will materialize that are just as inevitably inherent in the new technologies being developed. To illustrate this trade-off by means of an example: One of the main reasons why most of today's internet giants are based in California's Silicon Valley is a US law dating back to 1996. This law protects online platform operators (to a large extent) from being held responsible for content posted by platform users.[3] The aim of this piece of legislation was to demarcate clearly different spheres of responsibility, to preserve freedom of expression and diversity of opinion, and no doubt also to promote an emerging economic sector. However, in the eyes of its critics, this law increasingly operates as a kind of "carte blanche" for the unbridled dissemination of harmful content, with little fear of the consequences.[4] That now drives a debate about whether or not it is appropriate to retain this law unchanged.

Within Europe, much of the relevant regulation comes from the European Union. The EU takes a much more restrictive regulatory approach, in which the so-called precautionary principle plays a central role. According to the precautionary principle, dangers should from the outset be minimized as far as possible, and risks, whose extent and impact are difficult to assess up-front, ought to be avoided altogether. The EU's regulatory instruments relating to digitalization are currently springing up like mushrooms. They are so many and varied that it would go far beyond the scope of this contribution to provide even an initial overview. At the end of 2022, the European Parliament and the Council, following a proposal by the Commission, proclaimed a "digital decade" and adopted an ambitious policy program to provide comprehensive support for digital transformation in both the economy and within society by 2030.[5] Suffice it to mention and briefly address three specific areas.

First, there is general data law and data protection legislation, which deals with the collection, processing, storage, and use of personal data and—where applicable—other data. Traditional data protection legislation goes back to the second half of the 20th century and thus, as it were, to the digital Stone Age. However, it acquired a new dimension when the European General Data Protection Regulation (GDPR) came into force in 2018.[6] Data protection legislation applies regardless of whether the personal data concerned is collected, processed, stored, and used in conventional analogue form or in a digital format, but digital capture is now of course the norm. The GDPR has become quite prominently lodged in public consciousness, because when EU citizens access almost any website, they are first asked to what extent they consent to the collection and processing of their data (via cookies).[7] By contrast, most people are much less familiar with the new EU Data Act,[8] which was passed at the end of 2023 and is due to become fully applicable in September 2025. It regulates access, use and, where appropriate, the sharing of data (all data, but especially non-personal data) generated and collected in connection with the use of connected devices on the "Internet of Things", i.e. data generated, for instance, by "smart" household appliances. In addition to the EU-wide harmonization of data law, the Data Act is ultimately also concerned to regulate an emerging "data economy" and the data trading market.[9] As far as personal data is concerned, there evidently exists a degree of tension with the more restrictive data protection legislation. In theory, this is supposed to be resolved by the GDPR taking precedence in the event of a conflict, although many issues of detail still await resolution in practice.[10]

The second area of European regulation to be briefly discussed here also concerns the so-called "Digital Single Market". In 2022 two important new instruments were adopted which have been fully applicable since February 2024: the Digital Markets Act (DMA)[11] and the Digital Services Act (DSA).[12] They primarily serve to regulate platforms and set out mandatory guidelines for digital markets (such as Amazon or eBay) and digital services (such as Facebook or Instagram).[13] Their aim is to create a fair, open, and secure digital space which, on the one hand, protects platform users from economically and technologically superior platform operators and, on the other hand, ensures a level playing field of competition for all platforms operating within the European digital market.

In view of the fact that major online platforms can now effectively define entire new private law frameworks through their general terms and conditions, largely displacing the otherwise applicable statutory default regimes,[14] the establishment of such a level playing field is indeed urgently required.

The third and final example is the highly topical European AI Act which seeks to regulate artificial intelligence.[15] This initiative by the European Commission was adopted by the European Parliament shortly before the last legislative term ended in the spring of 2024 and, after approval by the Council, came into force in August 2024. Over the next couple of years, the AI Act will gradually become fully applicable. It may fairly be described as nothing less than the first attempt worldwide to channel the rapid development of artificial intelligence and give it a clear legal framework. At the heart of its regulatory approach lies the classification of AI systems into different categories of risk. Depending on the level of risk concerned, different rules apply. Accordingly, systems involving an unacceptably high risk (for example because they pose a threat to life and limb or result in human rights violations) are prohibited outright; in the case of all other systems, multi-tiered regulation determines what requirements must be met. For example, while

AI-enabled video games or spam filters are almost free from regulation, the use of artificial intelligence in the area of critical infrastructure is classified as high-risk and is thus subject to very exacting standards.

III. PERSPECTIVES ON FUTURE REGULATION

All of the regulatory instruments mentioned above (and many more besides) were passed with the declared intention of seizing the opportunities of digitalization and using them as fruitfully as possible for the benefit of Europe, while simultaneously minimizing the associated risks. At the same time, the standards set by the EU are also exerting international influence indirectly, outside of their actual scope of application, on account of "spillover effects", whether through deliberate political pressure or simply the mechanisms of the market. This is often referred to as the "Brussels Effect".[16] There is, however, much debate about whether the European balancing act between "innovation friendliness" and risk management in the area of digitalization is well-measured and will succeed in every respect, and especially how viable its chosen approaches will prove in practice.

At present, a particularly virulent debate is developing on the subject of the new AI Act. While European institutions like to highlight their pioneering role in regulating artificial intelligence, many others fear that local start-ups will become less competitive and that the Act will result in the creation of a bureaucratic monster. It is particularly the legal uncertainty associated with the new legislation that raises suspicions of inhibiting innovation rather than promoting it. According to media reports, even the chief architect of the European AI Act has now admitted that the "regulatory bar maybe has been set too high" and that it puts small European companies at a disadvantage when compared with the major US tech giants.[17]

When it comes to preventive (*ex ante*) regulation relating to brand-new technologies, a question that always arises is whether the legislator is actually in a position to obtain a sufficient overview over potential future developments, in order to steer them effectively and in the right direction. Regulating as it were "in the dark" does not seem helpful or indeed appropriate. While challenges and problems in field of data protection were, for instance, already quite well understood when the then German Federal Data Protection Act came into force in the late 1970s and when the first European Data Protection Directive (now replaced by the GDPR) was issued in 1995,[18] and while online markets and social networks were also known and relatively predictable when the DMA and the DSA were drafted to deal with them, the EU's regulation of AI is breaking new ground at a very early stage. As has rightly been pointed out, even without the existence of the AI Act, the rapid development in the area of artificial intelligence would not proceed in a legal vacuum, but would rather have to comply with all relevant requirements imposed by existing regulatory frameworks upon whose scope of application the AI system necessarily touches.[19] These frameworks range from product safety regulation and downstream product liability (for example in the case of smart household appliances), via Europe's extremely high standards in general consumer protection law (all of which must of course also be observed in the context of AI, for example when using chatbots), to the data protection rules within the GDPR and other instruments. Incidentally, there is now also a debate—quite independently of the AI Act—about whether and, if so, under what circumstances it is legally permissible to use copyrighted works in order to "train" artificial intelligence, also known as "data mining".[20]

In light of the above, it is no surprise to see leading regulatory experts arguing that, when it comes to artificial intelligence, it may be preferable for the time being to rely on "*ex post* liability rather than regulation *ex ante*".[21] Were hitherto unknown or hard-to-assess risks to materialize in the future, this would ensure that those affected are adequately compensated. At the same time, it would already at this stage provide a strong economic incentive for AI developers to minimize the risks associated with autonomous systems as far as possible. A proposal for a European AI Liability Directive,[22] first published in 2022, was however recently withdrawn from the legislative process.[23]

Yet "*ex post* regulation", using a subsequent liability regime to steer developments, also raises a number of questions and perspectives.[24] One particularly noteworthy example deserves special attention in the present context. For some years now the idea has been making the rounds amongst lawyers that, in addition to natural persons (i.e. individuals) and traditional "legal persons" (such as corporations), "electronic persons" ("e-persons" for short) should in future also be recognized as new subjects to which liability can attach.[25] This would (supposedly) make it easier to assign legal responsibility for loss or damage arising, for instance, where accidents are caused by self-driving cars or other autonomous agents. The "e-person" would then of course need to be provided with its own assets to act as a liability fund (a kind of minimum capital, potentially increased by "commissions" for the services which the "e-person" provides and supplemented by its own liability insurance).

It remains to be seen whether this development will in due course actually necessitate accident victims claiming directly from "e-persons" and taking them to court if needs be. Not every new technology requires a fundamentally new legal regime to deal with it. Critics of the "e-person" proposal have a point in arguing that the challenges posed by autonomous systems can also be met using more traditional legal means. Private law as it stands already contains sufficient mechanisms for attributing the actions of "e-persons" to the corporations or individuals standing behind them (in particular their manufacturers or operators) and thus to hold the latter accountable in the conventional way.[26] This more conventional way of claiming compensation would also create incentives for manufacturers and operators not to treat the "e-person" as a liability shield, but to design autonomous systems that are as safe as possible from the outset and then carefully monitor their ongoing operation.[27]

IV. THE UNDERESTIMATED SIGNIFICANCE OF "DIGITAL INCLUSION"

Finally, it is worth highlighting an aspect that has unfortunately hitherto proved a blind spot in the regulation of our increasingly digitalized world. The issue may be described as one of "digital inclusion" or "inclusiveness".

While "inclusion" or "inclusiveness" is a field with many facets, the present concern is not with how digitalization can help promote social inclusiveness in general terms, for instance by using modern technology to make up for physical disabilities, a process that could be described as "inclusion *through* digitalization". Nor is the concern here with "inclusion *into* digitalization", i.e., reducing barriers to accessing the digital world, for instance through the provision of tablet computers in schools so as to enable socially disadvantaged students easy everyday access to new media forms. Both aforementioned forms of inclusion are enormously important and pose significant challenges, some of which have already become the focus of regulation. For example, there is an EU Web Accessibility Directive specifically encouraging websites and mobile applications run by public bodies to promote "digital accessibility" on the internet.[28]

A survey of existing instruments gives the impression that the authorities in charge are not only (rightly) taking the rapid process of digitalization and its long-term continuation for granted, but that they are also (wrongly) taking for granted that all the citizens can and want to keep up with it at the same rapid pace. In Germany, an estimated 20 percent of people still do not have a smartphone and some do not even have a computer or email account; amongst people of retirement age, the proportion was still over 50 percent in 2021.[29] Although it can be assumed that the number of people living purely "analogue" lives will steadily dwindle and that assistance with "inclusion *into* digitalization" will contribute towards this, it should be an equally urgent concern of the state and/ or the EU to guarantee what may be called "inclusion *despite* digitalization" for those who, for whatever reason, are "lagging behind" in terms of technological development.

To illustrate the problem: It is now quite common for people to have to arrange appointments with, for example, public authorities purely online, by choosing a slot and providing an email address. The applicant must then first click on a link sent by email in order to identify themselves and to confirm the appointment, before receiving a QR code through a second email, which they can then use to "check in" on the day of the appointment. In some European countries with well-established national mobile payment systems (for example the Swedish payment app called Swish), people without a local bank account and a state-registered personal identity number are unable to visit certain cafés or restaurants because the latter no longer accept payments in cash or by card. Similarly, in Germany the popular flat-rate public transport ticket (*Deutschlandticket*), when issued by Deutsche Bahn, the main rail operator, is now only available in digital format.

Examples of this kind are ubiquitous but have so far appeared to have remained almost entirely off the regulatory radar. They are evidence of a lack of "inclusion *despite* digitalization". Yet without some form of support, many citizens are simply no longer able to navigate the digitized everyday life around them, to participate independently in society, or even to use essential infrastructure. Their "problem" is that they are "lagging behind" modern technology. The very use of such phrases acknowledges that some of those concerned may find themselves in this position involuntarily, for example for lack of funds, but at the same time it suggests that other affected citizens are lazy or unwilling to keep step with technological progress and thus have only themselves to blame. But it is not all that simple. While a society may legitimately be entitled to expect a certain level of pro-active integration on the part of its members (for example, even without a corresponding legal obligation, one can nowadays assume that everyone has a current account and access to a telephone connection), it is still part of each and every individual's self-determination, i.e. their freedom in leading an autonomous life, quite consciously to remain in "analogue" mode for longer than others. There is, in short, no generally accepted measure for the objectively "right" pace of digitalization. What is technically possible may well happen and be enthusiastically embraced by many, but at the same time it is absolutely essential to ensure that significant sections of society do not fall by the wayside.

A conceivable—if slightly crude— objection to the above argument is that the phenomenon described is no more than a "transitional problem" which will at some point resolve itself. But that is not true. In reality the problem will just shift and keep recurring in new shapes. Today's "digital natives"—"Generation Z" or the new "Generation Alpha"—will no doubt at some point no longer be able or willing to keep up with every technological development yet to come. We should therefore be thinking about long-term regulatory strategies that ensure a minimum level of economic, political, and social participation for everyone, even for people who are "lagging behind" technologically. Interestingly, there has for many years been a settled expectation that manufacturers of machines or electrical appliances must stock essential spare parts for a certain period of time after production of a given series has come to an end, so that customers are later on still in a position to have their devices repaired. As recently as in the summer of 2024, the existing EU Ecodesign Directive was replaced by a new European Ecodesign Regulation,[30] which requires the continued availability of spare parts throughout Europe for (in most cases) at least ten years, all in the interests of ecological sustainability. Should we then not, in the interest of a sustainable social development towards the brave new digital world, also require a sufficiently generous "access period" for individuals who are not at the cutting edge of technology?

Notes

1. See, for example, Gabriele Balbi, *The Digital Revolution: A Short History of an Ideology* (Oxford: OUP, 2023); Anthony Elliott, *The Culture of AI: Everyday Life and the Digital Revolution* (London: Routledge, 2019).

2. "Pause Giant AI Experiments: An Open Letter", March 22, 2023, https://futureoflife.org/open-letter/pause-giant-ai-experiments/ (accessed March 18, 2025). See also the criticism as summarized by Kari Paul et al., "Letter signed by Elon Musk demanding AI research pause sparks controversy" in *The Guardian*, April 1, 2023.

3. 47 U.S. Code § 230, as inserted by the Communications Decency Act (CDA) 1996.

4. For, the example, the dissenting opinion by Judge Lewis in the case of *Doe v. American Online Inc.*, 783 So. 2d 1010, esp. 1019 (Florida, 2001): "Through the majority's interpretation, the so-called 'Decency Act' has, contrary to well-established legal principles, been transformed from an appropriate shield into a sword of harm and extreme danger which places technology buzz words and economic considerations above the safety and general welfare of our people. I suggest that by interpreting the statute to provide this carte blanche immunity for wrongful conduct plainly not intended by Congress, the majority view ignores the common law underpinnings of the present controversy [...]".

5. Decision (EU) 2022/2481 of the European Parliament and of the Council of 14 December 2022 establishing the Digital Decade Policy Programme 2030, https://eur-lex.europa.eu/legal-content/ENG/TXT/PDF/?uri=CELEX:32022D2481 (accessed March 18, 2025).

6. Regulation (EU) 2016/679 of the European Parliament and of the Council of 27 April 2016 on the protection of natural persons with regard to the processing of personal data and on the free movement of such data, and repealing Directive 95/46/EC, https://eur-lex.europa.eu/legal-content/EN/TXT/PDF/?uri=CELEX:32016R0679 (accessed March 18, 2025).

7. Alongside the GDPR, the so-called ePrivacy Directive also plays a role here: Directive 2002/58/EC of the European Parliament and of the Council of 12 July 2002

concerning the processing of personal data and the protection of privacy in the electronic communications sector, https://eur-lex.europa.eu/legal-content/EN/TXT/PDF/?uri=CELEX:32002L0058 (accessed March 18, 2025).

8. Despite being described as an "Act", it is actually an EU legal instrument in the form of a Regulation: Regulation (EU) 2023/2854 of the European Parliament and of the Council of 13 December 2023 on harmonised rules on fair access to and use of data and amending Regulation (EU) 2017/2394 and Directive (EU) 2020/1828 (Data Act), https://eur-lex.europa.eu/legal-content/EN/TXT/PDF/?uri=OJ:L_202302854 (accessed March 18, 2025).

9. Alongside the Data Act, the so-called Data Governance Act also plays a major role here: Regulation (EU) 2022/868 of the European Parliament and of the Council of 30 May 2022 on European data governance and amending Regulation (EU) 2018/1724, https://eur-lex.europa.eu/legal-content/EN/TXT/PDF/?uri=CELEX:32022R0868 (accessed March 18, 2025).

10. See, for example, Frank Schemmel, "Data Act und DSGVO: Ziemlich beste Feinde?" in *Compliance Berater* (2024), pp. 301 ff.

11. Regulation (EU) 2022/1925 of the European Parliament and of the Council of 14 September 2022 on contestable and fair markets in the digital sector and amending Directives (EU) 2019/1937 and (EU) 2020/1828, https://eur-lex.europa.eu/legal-content/EN/TXT/PDF/?uri=CELEX:32022R1925 (accessed March 18, 2025).

12. Regulation (EU) 2022/2065 of the European Parliament and of the Council of 19 October 2022 on a Single Market For Digital Services and amending Directive 2000/31/EC, https://eur-lex.europa.eu/legal-content/EN/TXT/PDF/?uri=CELEX:32022R2065 (accessed March 18, 2025).

13. The DSA also provides for a certain liability privilege for third-party content. However, this is much narrower than

the one introduced in the US by the Communications Decency Act 1996 in § 230 (see n. 3 above and text thereto). Under the DSA, the liability privilege is limited by extensive due-diligence obligations of the online platform, combined with a so-called "notice and take down" procedure for illegal content.

14. See Florian Möslein, "Digitising Defaults: Methods and Mechanisms of Generating Default Rules in the Digital Age" in Birke Häcker and Johannes Ungerer (eds.), *Default Rules in Private Law* (Oxford: Hart Publishing, 2025).

15. Regulation (EU) 2024/1689 of the European Parliament and of the Council of 13 June 2024 laying down harmonised rules on artificial intelligence and amending Regulations (EC) No 300/2008, (EU) No 167/2013, (EU) No 168/2013, (EU) 2018/858, (EU) 2018/1139 and (EU) 2019/2144 and Directives 2014/90/EU, (EU) 2016/797 and (EU) 2020/1828 (Artificial Intelligence Act) https://eur-lex.europa.eu/legal-content/EN/TXT/PDF/?uri=OJ:L_202401689 (accessed March 18, 2025).

16. The expression appears to have been coined by Anu Bradford, "The Brussels Effect" in 107 *Northwestern University Law Review*, 1, pp. 1 ff. See also Anu Bradford, *The Brussels Effect: How the European Union Rules the World* (New York/Oxford: OUP, 2020), esp. Chapter 6 on "Digital Economy".

17. Lionel Laurent, "Europe Has US Tech in Its Sights. It Might Miss" in *Bloomberg Law*, August 1, 2024, https://news.bloomberglaw.com/artificial-intelligence/europe-has-us-tech-in-its-sights-it-might-miss-lionel-laurent (accessed March 18, 2025).

18. Directive 95/46/EC of 24 October 1995 on the protection of individuals with regard to the processing of personal data and on the free movement of such data https://eur-lex.europa.eu/legal-content/ENG/TXT/PDF/?uri=CELEX:31995L0046 (accessed March 18, 2025).

19. See, for example, Gerhard Wagner, "Künstliche Intelligenz – Die EU als globaler Regulierer?" in *FAZ*, March 4, 2024, p. 18.

20. In Germany, the first court decision on this issue was recently handed down by the Regional Court in Hamburg, Judgment of 27.9.2024 (ref. 310 O 227/23).

21. See, in particular, Wagner, "Künstliche Intelligenz" (n. 19), p. 18.

22. *Proposal for a Directive of the European Parliament and of the Council* on adapting non-contractual civil liability rules to artificial intelligence (AI Liability Directive) of 28.9.2022, https://eur-lex.europa.eu/legal-content/EN/TXT/PDF/?uri=CELEX:52022PC0496 (accessed March 18, 2025).

23. This was announced in February 2025: see https://commission.europa.eu/document/download/7617998c-86e6-4a74-b33c-249e8a7938cd_en?filename=COM_2025_45_1_annexes_EN.pdf as well as https://www.ai-liability-directive.com/ (both accessed March 18, 2025).

24. For a critique of the then-proposed version of the AI Liability Directive, see Gerhard Wagner, "Die Richtlinie über KI-Haftung: Viel Rauch, wenig Feuer" in *Juristenzeitung* (2023), pp. 123 ff.

25. The European Parliament already published such a proposal in 2017: European Parliament resolution of 16 February 2017 with recommendations to the Commission on Civil Law Rules on Robotics, para. 59 (f), https://www.europarl.europa.eu/doceo/document/TA-8-2017-0051_EN.html (accessed March 18, 2025). See also the contribution by Cornelius Kleiner, *Die elektronische Person* (Baden-Baden: Nomos, 2021).

26. See, for example, Thomas Riehm, "Nein zur ePerson! Gegen die Anerkennung einer digitalen Rechtspersönlichkeit" in *Recht Digital* (2020), pp. 42 ff.

___

27. Ibid., p. 48.

28. Directive (EU) 2016/2102 of the European Parliament and of the Council of 26 October 2016 on the accessibility of the websites and mobile applications of public sector bodies, https://eur-lex.europa.eu/legal-content/EN/TXT/PDF/?uri=CELEX:32016L2102 (accessed March 18, 2025).

29. Cf. Report of the German Association of Cities and Municipalities of June 3, 2021, https://www.dstgb.de/themen/digitalisierung/aktuelles/mehr-als-die-haelfte-der-ueber-65-jaehrigen-nutzt-kein-smartphone/ (accessed March 18, 2025).

30. Regulation (EU) 2024/1781 of the European Parliament and of the Council of 13 June 2024 establishing a framework for the setting of ecodesign requirements for sustainable products, amending Directive (EU) 2020/1828 and Regulation (EU) 2023/1542 and repealing Directive 2009/125/EC, https://eur-lex.europa.eu/legal-content/EN/TXT/PDF/?uri=OJ:L_202401781 (accessed March 18, 2025).

CHAPTER 10

PEACE AND SECURITY IN THE AGE OF GLOBAL STRATEGIC COMPETITION—CHALLENGES FOR EUROPE[1]

HANS-DIETER LUCAS

ZEITENWENDE—CHANGE OF PARADIGM IN EUROPE'S SECURITY ENVIRONMENT

"Nothing is the way it used to be"—that was a key message in Chancellor Scholz's famous speech on what he called the *Zeitenwende*, three days after Russia's attack on Ukraine on February 27, 2022.[2] Indeed, Russia's brutal war against Ukraine was and is the most striking sign that Europe has finally entered a new era. But the *Zeitenwende*, or epochal turning point, goes far beyond Russia's war against Ukraine. The *Zeitenwende* stands for an all-encompassing, transformative process which jeopardizes peace and security in and for Europe in an unprecedented manner. Europe is being confronted with a change of paradigm regarding its security environment which is manifesting itself in many ways:

- Europe is surrounded by a "ring of fire" consisting of conflicts that only start in Ukraine, then extend down to the Caucasus, run through the greater Middle East, across North Africa and into the Sahel region.

- While China remains a strategically important economic partner for Europe, it has also become a systemic rival and a competitor. That is also increasingly true in the field of security, as evidenced by Chinese support for Russia in the war against Ukraine. The participation of thousands of North Korean soldiers in this war underlines that Europe and the Indo-Pacific region are more and more intertwined.

- The international arms control regimes developed during and after the Cold War have to a great extent collapsed. At the same time, new disruptive, destabilizing technologies are emerging: cyber technology, AI, drones, space, and hypersonic weapons. And there is also the danger of nuclear proliferation in the Middle East should Iran succeed in developing a nuclear weapon.

- Hybrid warfare has become an important feature of geopolitical competition. Countries such as Russia try to undermine our societies through information warfare and cyberattacks against our critical infrastructure.

- As became clear during the COVID-19 pandemic, Europe's supply chains and thus its economic security are increasingly challenged due to its dependence on raw materials, energy, semiconductors, etc., which are critical to the functioning of its industries.

- The consequences of climate change—droughts, desertification, and other extreme weather events, as well as climate-induced migration—will very likely be the most important challenge to peace and security in the long run.

Four additional global trends further complicate this already worrisome scenario:

- A global power shift at the expense of Europe and the US: While new powers or groupings such as the BRICS play an ever more important role in world politics, the ability of the West to substantially influence, let alone control, developments of strategic importance is shrinking. The recent escalation in the Middle East is a case in point in that respect. While the EU and US share of the global population and world trade is steadily diminishing, the BRICS alone have already surpassed the G7 in terms of population and economic output. Finally, the number of countries that share the West's commitment to democracy and a liberal society is also shrinking.

- Intensified geopolitical and geo-economic competition: Russia's imperialist policy in Europe is the starkest example of this. At the same time, China is aspiring to replace the US as the leading global power by the late 2040s. With that in mind,

China is building up its military capabilities and displaying aggressive behavior in parts of the Indo-Pacific, for instance with regard to Taiwan as well as in the South China Sea. Despite their differences, China and Russia work together in what they call a "limitless partnership," which unites them in their opposition to the US and the principles the Political West represents. Both aim to change the world order in line with their interests. Other emerging powers such as India, Brazil, or Saudi Arabia are also striving for more influence, although clearly in different ways.

- The erosion of multilateralism and the rules-based international order: This development is evident above all in the weakness of the UN and the blockade of the UN Security Council—the key body responsible for fostering international peace and security—as well as the crisis in multilateral institutions such as the WTO or the G20.

- Finally, a tendency towards a diffusion of power is becoming apparent as non-state actors, multinational companies, and social media gain ever greater influence over world politics.

All these developments combined show that the paradigmatic change in Europe's security environment is multidimensional. That raises fundamental questions for Europe. How is Europe going to deal with these multiple security threats? Is enduring peace in Europe even possible?

How can Europe pursue its security interests beyond Europe, in particular with regard to China, as well as what is referred to as the Global South?

THE RUSSIAN THREAT TO EUROPEAN SECURITY

Today, Russia poses the most imminent threat to European security. Russia's goal is twofold: to destroy Ukraine as an independent, sovereign state, and to undermine NATO and the EU in a way that will cause these two major pillars of the Political West to eventually fail.

Russia's war against Ukraine is not only a classic territorial conflict between two countries, it also has a systemic dimension as Putin has identified the West as Russia's adversary. It is no coincidence that Russia is being supported by autocracies such as China, Iran, and North Korea. Hence, the outcome of this war will have major consequences for European security and beyond. If Putin wins in Ukraine, he will see this as an encouragement to continue his fight against European and Atlantic institutions. A Russian victory would probably also embolden other autocratic leaders to act in a similar way.

This makes supporting Ukraine as long as it is necessary, including militarily, a strategic imperative for the EU, the G7, and NATO. That is why Germany has become the second-largest provider of financial support and weapons to Ukraine after the US. NATO and the EU have always made it clear that they do not want to enter into a military conflict with Russia and that ultimately only a negotiated settlement between the parties can end this war. For the time being, however, an end to this bloody war is not in sight. So far, Putin has seemed prepared to countenance a peace dictated by Russia only on conditions that would be acceptable neither to Ukraine nor to the West.

Given Putin's long-term objectives, Russia will very likely remain an immediate security threat to Europe for at least as long as Putin is in power. There is no common ground with Putin's Russia regarding the basic principles of a long-lasting European, legitimate peace order. The Charter of Paris for a New Europe of 1990 contained the basic principles for a just and stable peace order for the whole of Europe, such as respect for national sovereignty and territorial integrity, democracy, human rights, and the rule of law. All countries within the Euro-Atlantic area, including Russia, signed this Charter. Today Russia would certainly not agree to the obligations set out in this document. Putin's vision of Europe is an imperialist one, with an enlarged Russia and a huge zone of influence for Russia based on the principle of "might makes right." He is pursuing this vision by waging war against Ukraine, as well as through a massive military build-up and hybrid activities against EU Member States and NATO allies.[3]

Against this background—the lack of prospects for a European settlement and sustained Russian revisionism—strong defense and deterrence will be needed for the foreseeable future. At its recent summits in Vilnius and Washington, NATO made far-reaching decisions in order to prioritize deterrence and defense, improving its defense readiness as well as strengthening its Eastern flank.

EUROPEAN RESPONSES

Europe must adapt not only to Russia's aggressive behavior but to a whole range of other threats to its security. At the same time, this need to adapt is all the more urgent as it has become clear over the last few years that the main guarantor of European security, the US, will not engage in the same way in conflicts in and around Europe as was the case in the past. Instead, the US will concentrate more on China and the Indo-Pacific, both in terms of political focus and military deployments. Furthermore, it is unclear in the immediate aftermath of the US presidential elections how the future Trump Administration intends to shape relations with Europe in the sphere of security policy and what role the US will play in NATO in the years to come. At any rate, Donald Trump made it clear during his electoral campaign that he expects Europeans to spend much more on their defense and assume greater responsibility for their own security.

For Europeans that means two things:

• They need to massively increase their military capabilities with a twofold aim: to contribute more substantially to collective defense within NATO, thus strengthening its European pillar and enabling the EU to take military action if necessary.

- They also need to improve the EU's ability to pursue a more effective and coordinated foreign and security policy.

With regard to military capabilities, Europeans have neglected them since the end of the Cold War, whereas Russia has already been investing massively in modernizing its military for a number of years. Since 2014, after the annexation of Crimea by Russia, Europeans have turned the trend around and increased defense spending considerably. A total of twenty-three NATO allies now spend a minimum of 2 percent of their GDP on defense—among them, for the first time in many years, Germany.

But as industrial capacities are still limited, it will take years before increased defense spending results in new tanks, ships, drones, or aircraft in the necessary quality and quantity. When Germany's Defense Minister Boris Pistorius demands that the Bundeswehr must become ready for war—or *kriegstüchtig*—within the coming five years, then that means two things: first, that the possibility of a military conflict with Russia can no longer be ruled out; and second, that Europe's armed forces do not have the necessary capabilities to deter Russia or to prevail in a conflict. Part of the picture is that vis-à-vis the nuclear superpower

Russia, Europe essentially relies on the extended nuclear guarantee it is given by the US, even though the independent nuclear forces of France and the UK contribute to NATO's nuclear deterrence. That is why Europeans have a vital interest in a strong, reliable transatlantic relationship.

A balanced transatlantic relationship in the defense sphere necessitates fair burden-sharing between Europe and the US when it comes to providing capabilities within NATO. And more and better European capabilities are necessary to enable the EU to take military action if and when necessary.

This requires more capable European defense industries. In concrete terms, Europe must step up the joint production and procurement of military goods and find the necessary financial resources for this. Only then can Europe overcome the costly fragmentation of its defense industries. Europe does not need five different types of battle tanks when the US has just one. In recent years, the EU has taken a number of important steps towards stronger European defense through initiatives such as Permanent Structured Cooperation (PESCO), the creation of the European Defense Fund, and the European Peace Facility. For the first time in its history, the European Commission will have a commissioner responsible for the defense industries. These are all encouraging steps, but given the major threats Europe is facing, it needs to speed up.

At the same time, the EU needs to improve its decision-making mechanisms. It reacted quickly to Russia's aggression against Ukraine when it decided to end its energy dependency on Russia within months, as well as to impose massive sanctions on Russia and support Ukraine economically and militarily in an unprecedented fashion. However, all decisions in the EU in the field of foreign and security policy are still being taken on the basis of unanimity, with all twenty-seven Member States having to agree. There is always the danger that one Member State might block major decisions, including in times of crisis. Such a blockade would be even more likely in an enlarged European Union of thirty-five Member States. That is why the German government, together with others, supports the introduction of qualified majority voting in the sphere of foreign and security policy within the framework of the existing treaties. EU enlargement is a geostrategic necessity if the EU does not want the Western Balkans as well as Ukraine, Moldova, and possibly Georgia to fall within the sphere of influence of either Russia or China. Thus, EU enlargement also has a strong security policy dimension. But in order to be successful, EU enlargement needs to go hand in hand with institutional reforms.

INTEGRATED SECURITY AND THE IMPORTANCE OF THE GLOBAL SOUTH[4]

Strengthening its defense can only be one key element as Europe tries to secure peace and stability. That is why Germany's National Security Strategy speaks about "integrated security" as the overarching concept that guides its security policy.[5] Integrated security means combining diplomatic, economic, and military tools in order to confront multiple challenges, including threats such as cyber, information, and hybrid warfare.

Such an approach will also be necessary when addressing security challenges arising from a multipolar world characterized by geostrategic competition. This is particularly relevant with regard to China as well as what is referred to as the Global South. While remaining a hugely important economic partner, China poses more and more challenges to Europe's security. It supports Russia politically and is delivering dual-use goods which Russia uses for its war economy. China is developing its own military at great speed, and it is behind malicious cyber and hybrid activities against Western countries.

As a consequence, Europe has to adapt to a China that has been changing a lot in recent years. That does not mean decoupling from China. After all, China will play a decisive role in the global economy of the 21st century as well as in the fight against climate change. But—as the German China Strategy puts it[6]—Europe needs to reduce one-sided strategic dependencies and to de-risk by diversifying, for example when it comes to sourcing raw materials, making investments, but also protecting its critical infrastructure. The decision taken by the German Government to do without Huawei and ZTE components in critical German digital infrastructure highlights the fact that Germany is increasingly aware of the necessity to de-risk its relationship with China.

Europe also needs to find an answer to China's and Russia's growing influence in the Global South, meaning countries outside the traditional Western world. The Global South has become a hugely important field of geostrategic competition, mainly due to Russia's and China's behavior. Whereas Russia is focusing on establishing military presences, China is trying to expand its influence over these countries, for instance by developing close economic and infrastructural ties—quite literally with its Belt and Road Initiative. Unlike the EU, China provides loans without raising good governance issues, which gives China a comparative advantage.

Africa is a case in point: China replaced Europe as Africa's most important trading partner quite some time ago. And Russia has established a very substantial military presence in the Sahel region. At the same time, Europe, and in particular France, has had to reduce or even abandon its military presence there.

Given Europe's vital political and economic interests in Africa as well in the Global South, it must not leave these regions to China or Russia. It is in Europe's interest that countries outside the Political West defend fundamental principles of the UN Charter such as sovereignty and territorial integrity. The difficult negotiations at the UN General Assembly to win broad support for resolutions condemning Russia's aggression showed how challenging this is. Many countries have a different view of this conflict, maintaining that this war in Europe is essentially a European problem, that they do not want to be drawn into a conflict between the West and Russia, or be forced to choose between the West on the one hand and Russia and China on the other.

As a consequence, Europe needs to reach out to the Global South in a more coordinated, strategic way. This applies in particular to those countries that are able to shape the future international order and that share Europe's commitment to basic principles of international law. Such outreach requires dialogue on an equal footing and a readiness to listen with an open mind. Even if many countries of the Global South are critical of the West for many reasons—Western "double standards" being one of them—and do not share all its values, it is possible to build partnerships around themes of common interest, such as climate change, energy, or infrastructure. Such a "realistic" approach focuses less on differences regarding values and more on trying to identify overlapping interests. With this in mind, the G7 has, based on a German initiative, launched a Partnership for Global Investment and Infrastructure, which will mobilize 600 billion US dollars by 2027 for major infrastructure projects. The EU has committed to contributing to this endeavor through its Global Gateway initiative. These initiatives are not only about development aid; they are driven by mutual interests. They aim to create win-win situations, to facilitate the creation of value and jobs in these countries and bind them closer to the G7 and the EU.

Trade is another important bridge between the EU and the Global South. That requires an open, not a protectionist EU trade policy. The conclusion of FTAs with partners around the globe such as MERCOSUR is a powerful tool in that respect.

PRIORITIZING SECURITY AND THE NECESSITY OF A NEW MINDSET

In conclusion, four points seem to be particularly important for the future debate on Europe's security:

1. We are living in a world that is much more volatile than anything we have seen since the end of World War II. A new, stable world order or long-lasting peace and stability in Europe are unfortunately not in sight. Although the basic principles of a peaceful world order are well-known and enshrined in the UN Charter, there is no "guardian" of the international order, no single power, organization, or group of nations that is able or willing to enforce the implementation of these principles globally[7]—in particular territorial integrity as a key precondition for a more peaceful and stable international system.[8]

2. Europeans will not be able to change that. But they must uphold these principles and build alliances with partners around the globe in order to defend these tenets. At the same time, Europe must be prepared to master the challenges resulting from an extremely unstable and volatile security environment.

Whether or not Europe succeeds in this endeavor will, to a large extent, depend on its mindset.[9] It needs a stronger awareness of the extraordinary threats to its security and to its way of life. As President Macron has put it: "Notre Europe est mortelle" [our Europe is mortal].[10] A new mindset must also be based on clarity as to where Europe sees itself in the decades to come—as a center of power, a pole in a multipolar world able to defend its interests, or a kind of political and economic province.

Many people in Europe still think that at some stage we will return to the seemingly comfortable situation we lived in until a couple of years ago. That will not be the case. In this respect, what in German is called a *Ruck* is needed in Europe's political and public debates—something that jolts us awake and refocuses our discussions.

3. In his speech at the 2024 Munich Security Conference, Chancellor Scholz said: "Ohne Sicherheit

ist alles nichts"[11] [without security, all else is nothing]. If security is so vitally important, it needs to be prioritized. The German National Security Strategy talks about the necessity to become *wehrhaft*, in other words the need to be able to defend ourselves. That requires proactive diplomacy as the first line of defense. In an age of intensified geopolitical competition, diplomacy will be needed to balance diverging interests and avoid escalation as well as conflict. In order to assert itself, Europe will also need economic strength based on competitive industries and innovation. In that respect, Mario Draghi is right when he highlights the nexus between security and economic as well as technological performance in his ground-breaking report to the European Council on Europe's competitiveness.

But given the fact that Europe will be confronted with very concrete, military security challenges for the foreseeable future, it also needs a strong deterrence and defense. Of course, there is a price tag to this. However, it should not be forgotten that during the Cold War, the Federal Republic of Germany spent 3 percent and more on defense. That was largely accepted by its population, and West Germany was not a poor country back then. But finding the necessary public support—and the funds—for significantly increased defense spending over many years to come will present a key challenge for European governments.

4. *Wehrhaftigkeit* requires resilience in a double sense:

- First, with regard to our critical infrastructure, our supply chains for energy and raw materials as well as the information space. Building these resiliences is a key task, above all for national governments, but also for the EU. The more resilient Europe is economically and technologically, the less vulnerable it will be.

- Second, Europe needs what one might call "inner resilience," meaning cohesion based on key values and principles—democracy, the rule of law, and human rights. That is what Europe is, and it should be clear about it.

Resilience also requires unity when it comes to countering external threats. Carl von Clausewitz, the founding father of modern strategic thinking, reminded us that unity and cohesion are the center of gravity of any alliance. While Putin's Russia and others try to undermine Western societies and sow division, unity within the EU, NATO, and the G7 are key. Fragmentation is one of the biggest threats to Europe's security.

It was European and transatlantic unity and unwavering commitment to the ideas and principles binding us together, including the rejection of narrow-minded nationalism as well as resolve and joint action, that proved essential in ensuring that the West prevailed during the Cold War. Heeding this basic lesson will be vital if we are to master the great challenges ahead.

Notes

1. This article represents the personal view of the author.

2. Speech by Chancellor Olaf Scholz on February 27, 2022 at the German Bundestag, https://www.bundesregierung. de/breg-en/search/policy-statement-by-olaf-scholz-chancellor-of-the-federal-republic-of-germany-and-member-of-the-german-bundestag-27-february-2022-in-berlin-2008378 (accessed December 3, 2024).

3. For Russia's hybrid activities against Germany, see Arndt Freytag von Loringhoven and Leon Erlenhorst, *Putins Angriff auf Deutschland: Desinformation, Propaganda, Cyberattacken* (Berlin: Econ Verlag, 2024).

4. The notion of the Global South, however widely used, is controversial for a number of reasons. See, for instance, Tobias Berger, "The 'Global South' as a Relational Category—Global Hierarchies in the Production of Law and Legal Pluralism" in *Third World Quarterly*, 42(9), 2021, pp. 2001–2017.

5. *Integrated Security for Germany. National Security Strategy*, https://www.nationalesicherheitsstrategie.de/en.html (accessed December 3, 2024).

6. Strategy on China of the Government of the Federal Republic of Germany, https://www.auswaertiges-amt.de/resource/blob/2608578/810fdade376b1467f20bdb697b2acd58/china-strategie-data.pdf (accessed December 3, 2024).

7. Various options for a stable world are discussed extensively in Herfried Münkler, *Welt in Aufruhr. Die Ordnung der Mächte im 21. Jahrhundert* (Berlin: Rowohlt Verlag, 2023).

8. On the centrality of the principle of territorial integrity for maintaining peace see, for example, Jürgen Osterhammel, "Weltordnung und Friedensstiftung seit 1945" in Michael Rutz (ed.), *Krieg! Und Frieden?* (Freiburg: Herder Verlag, 2023), pp. 17–47.

9. This argument is made, for instance, by former Finnish President Sauli Niinistö, Special Advisor to the President of the European Commission, in his report "Safer Together. Strengthening Europe's Civilian and Military Preparedness and Readiness," October 2024, https://commission.europa.eu/document/download/5bb2881f-9e29-42f2-8b77-8739b19d047c_en?filename=2024_Niinisto-report_Book_VF.pdf (accessed December 3, 2024).

10. Speech by President Emmanuel Macron at the Sorbonne, April 25, 2024, https://www.elysee.fr/en/emmanuel-macron/2024/04/24/europe-speech (accessed December 3, 2024).

11. Speech by Chancellor Olaf Scholz at the MSC, February 17, 2024, https://www.bundeskanzler.de/bk-en/news/speech-by-federal-chancellor-olaf-scholz-at-the-munich-security-conference-2260378 (accessed December 3, 2024).

CHAPTER 11

COMMON SENSE IN OUR WORLD

TIMO MEYNHARDT

The call for more common sense is a recurring topic, and a lack of it often bemoaned when it comes to political and economic decisions or government regulation. We might ask, where is common sense to be found? Common sense is itself often the object of serious criticism: Is someone using common sense as a way of claiming their own beliefs to be correct or simply offering platitudes as supposed solutions?[1] So what does sound judgment or universal reason mean today?

In uncertain times in particular when guidance is in short supply, the easily understandable advice provided by common sense is very welcome. It includes the promise of bringing clarity to confusing situations, exposing implausible views, and finding pragmatic solutions. This ranges from everyday adages ("the proof of the pudding is in the eating") via aphorisms ("talk is silver, silence is golden") to profound worldly wisdom ("nothing is true without its opposite"). It is clear that the realm of common sense—like a kind of cultural meme—has developed empirical values that prove useful and are passed on down the generations.

But in a highly complex society that demands nuanced answers, which can overwhelm all of us, what does common sense have to offer? We have to set priorities, filter information, and justify our actions to others. This has always been the case, but it applies even more so in situations that fundamentally affect our self-image and our options for action as individuals. At the moment, this particularly affects the consequences of climate change and the impact of artificial intelligence. What role can the thought processes of everyday pragmatism play when people are behaving in ways that threaten their own living conditions on Earth? Can we use practical wisdom to keep up with the rapid development of artificial intelligence? The great advantage of common sense is precisely that it offers guidance in times of uncertainty. So, let's have more common sense going forward? Yes, but...

In the following essay, I would like to argue for a reinforcement and extension of the basic idea that we humans are capable of developing an understanding of causal effects, human motivations and behaviors and, more generally, of relationships in the world without conscious thought and without any effort—intuitively, as it were—and are able to act rationally on this basis.

A LITTLE LOOK BACK

For centuries, common sense has been brought into play when practical reason and suitability for everyday use are required. An idea, a decision, or an action should be immediately understandable to a normal ("common") adult of average development with a natural capacity for judgment. On closer inspection, however, such a demand is contingent on many factors and therefore also easy to criticize. But time and again it seems to prove its worth. For example, since the Victorian era, English courts have used the fictional figure of "the man on the Clapham omnibus" to ask how a reasonable person would have behaved in a certain situation.

Adam Smith, the Scottish moral philosopher and founder of classical economics, created his concept of the "impartial spectator" to a similar end.[2]

The introduction of fictional people as reference points to test reasonableness is a secular version of the religious question of a God-fearing life. In both cases, a change or broadening of perspective is intended to provide better guidance and thus make it easier to find the right path. Fundamentally, it is always about the extent to which a person can trust their immediate sense of perception. In "common sense philosophy," as first developed by Thomas Reid (1764),[3] this question is answered in the positive. In psychology, this approach lives on as "common sense psychology."[4] Not without a certain degree of value judgment, this perspective is also referred to as naive or even lay psychology. Here we should draw a distinction between expert knowledge and the rationally based search for truth and knowledge and mere everyday understanding. It seems almost paradoxical: We pursue scientifically proven knowledge and yet cannot do without common sense, which is not always correct but is often astonishingly effective. In complex situations especially, common sense, which comes across as completely unscientific, can create clarity and order.

To the extent we can trace it back, common sense is derived from the Latin expression *sensus communis*, which in turn is probably a translation of the Greek *koine aisthesis* from Aristotle's theory of perception. It assumes a kind of general sense in which perceptual impressions come together to create an overall impression. Later, a wide variety of levels of meaning and concepts were added: ordinary understanding, sense of community, natural judgment, and shared knowledge. What has remained to this day is the emphasis on integrating initially unconnected elements into a holistic perception or form.

Over the centuries, the original idea of *koine aisthesis* has become increasingly refined and applied to various aspects of human perception, judgment, and ultimately human abilities. This ranges from simple sensory-motor stimulus-response relationships (for example the intuitive avoidance of danger) to the highest forms of moral judgment (for example weighing up ethical dilemmas). Soon the question arose of how collectively shared bodies of knowledge in which common sense is culturally anchored are created. Today, the mechanisms that spontaneously create order in psychological and social systems are discussed in modern theories of self-organization.[5]

At least three main points can be identified in this
many-faceted debate. *First*, it examines the extent to
which this is an unconscious (implicit) or conscious
(explicit) ability. *Second*, the connection between individual experience and collectively shared beliefs is
repeatedly discussed. *Third*, the question arises as to
what role subjective assessments play in common sense.

This last aspect in particular leads directly to the
issue of common sense's fundamental abilities. It is
applicable when it proves to be useful or meaningful.
This applies in all cases where there is no single truth
and at best a common interpretation can be found that
is acceptable to as many people as possible. Common
sense, on the other hand, is clearly inapplicable when
there is one fundamental solution to a problem that is
considered appropriate, true, and reasonable, regardless of whether individual people can agree with it.
Psychological research provides ample evidence of the
conditions under which intuition offers good advice
and when it does not.[6]

This also reveals the Janus-faced nature of common
sense. It can quickly turn out to be a cognitive distortion when applied to issues in the objective world that
go beyond immediate everyday experience. In a situation of immediate danger in road traffic, a person
can react correctly using their intuition. By contrast,

people find it almost impossible to intuitively grasp physical or chemical processes of climate change or the construction of Large Language Models (LLM) in AI technology. The limits of immediate, intuitive perception also become apparent in the social world. When is something a banal truism and when is it an example of profound wisdom?[7]

Common sense as a collective treasure trove of experience has remained fairly robust over time and thrives as a result of its self-actualization in different eras. So nothing is necessarily added, but rather previous experiences are applied in new contexts. In this respect, it does not indicate a lack of epistemological progress if, for example, the results of modern research into attitudes sound hardly any different in their basic statements than the recommendations of rhetoric teachers from two thousand years ago.

Is this kind of evolutionary updating enough in today's world? Do we need new standards for assessing how we live with artificial intelligence, which could, for example, be asked to analyze feelings and react empathetically to a person? The same question about the usefulness of common sense as it currently exists arises in the case of people's ability to adapt to climate change, for example when it comes to the significant increase in the pace of transformation that is necessary from a scientific point of view.

In my opinion, there are at least three arguments in favor of society making efforts to reinforce and develop common sense.

I. COMMON SENSE CAN HELP US WHEN WE LACK PRECISE KNOWLEDGE

Without instinctive, intuitive access to our environment and to ourselves, we would be unable to act. We must be able to trust that gravity always works, even if we cannot explain it ourselves. It is exactly the same with many other everyday experiences. It's the only way we can achieve reliability and stability. This seems trivial, but it is by no means the case when we simply consider how challenging it is to explain gravity scientifically, in which case common sense often provides only very rough clues in the shape of metaphors or proverbs. However, such concision usually contains a proven trans-situational insight that must remain imprecise and associative precisely in order to address that diffuse motivational and emotional hinterland inside us that we are hardly aware of and that is difficult to access linguistically.

Sometimes, even in the rigorous natural sciences, the cognitive process itself remains obscure and can only be explained by an intuitive approach. Of course, this form of creativity is often subject to a long research process involving failures and every solution can only claim provisional validity. Anyone wanting to follow the winding paths of common sense should also prepare themselves for long periods of fruitless work and even be prepared to pursue doubts, counterfactual intuition, or simply a gut feeling.

For example, there is a letter from Albert Einstein in which he explains to a friend how he arrives at theoretical statements intuitively from observations. In the letter, Einstein uses terms such as "extralogical sphere," "pragmatic," and "non-logical nature."[8] In this context the idea of a flash of inspiration is not so far-fetched. Such cognitive strategies that cannot be derived or deduced by the logic of induction can be easily traced not just in Einstein's work but also in that of other great scientists such as Isaac Newton or Charles Darwin.[9]

What applies to science should also guide us in everyday life: The source of new, viable solutions does not necessarily have to be well-founded, as long as they feel right to us and are coherent for other people. However, it is then important to estimate the effects and impacts as rationally as possible.[10] Without this second step, we run the risk of asserting something that knowledge is fundamentally (better) able to tell us. Such an interpretation of common sense is a key feature of populist arguments. Again, it does not apply to those areas where basically no correct solution can be found, such as when evaluating the consequences of climate policies or regulating artificial intelligence. It is precisely here that we can see clearly whether someone accepts the limits of common sense or is abusing it in a populist way and claiming something as truth that is ultimately just a subjective assessment.

If we fail to make an intellectually sophisticated solution accessible to everyday understanding, we should not be surprised if it is not seen as acceptable. The resulting mistrust cannot be eliminated using yet more factual arguments. Either the solution must be rejected or the resources of common sense should be used in a better way. New ideas in the economic, technological, and social world in particular should be subjected to this common-sense test in order to avoid accusations that they lack a connection to reality, are rarefied or elitist. One of the greatest strengths of common sense is its ability to challenge the everyday comprehensibility of grandiose abstractions.

The explosive issue of dealing with complexity lies in the nature of the challenges themselves. It is always important to distinguish whether the answers to questions can lead to fundamentally unambiguous solutions or if such answers always lead only to fundamentally ambiguous solutions. In the first instance, factual knowledge (logic, rigorous argument, etc.) is required; in the second instance, we need values-based knowledge (emotion, motivation, etc.).[11] The former aims to produce value-free statements such as those issued by the natural sciences which define their epistemological progress. The latter comprise statements that can never be unambiguous due to their intrinsic need for interpretation. In practice, these different types of knowledge are often closely linked. Common sense suggests we should not play them off against each other.

Today we have good, reliable evidence about the consequences of global warming and environmental pollution. It is much more difficult to find innovative ways of collective adaptation that chime with everyday rationality. The same applies to understanding the incalculable possibilities of artificial intelligence. In both cases we must resort to the practical wisdom of first and foremost not doing things whose consequences we cannot foresee. At the same time, we must recognize that we are in a process of investigation that takes time. In this respect, we are now particularly dependent on common sense and its development, which acts as a corrective to supposedly simple solutions to complex problems and at the same time does not overestimate its own range of application.

II. COMMON SENSE STRENGTHENS THE COMPETENCE OF THE PUBLIC GOOD

Over time, in the German-speaking world, "gesunder Menschenverstand" became the accepted translation of "common sense."[12] Today, this almost seems like a definition of *sensus communis*, whereas the first translation of Thomas Reid's seminal work still talked about "gemeiner Menschenverstand."

More important for our purposes, however, is the more comprehensive use of the concept, which has been liberated from the original idea of *koine aisthesis*. What interests me about common sense is less the question of developing a sensory-motor stimulus-response relationship, but rather how the integration of value judgments can give rise to something that is considered reasonable to the benefit of the common good. When it comes to coexistence in society, it is also about integrating needs.[13]

In this context, Immanuel Kant's three maxims for the use of common sense are groundbreaking.[14] He calls the first "thinking for oneself," by which he means independent, unbiased thinking. In the second maxim, "think from the standpoint of everyone else," he calls for a position when forming judgments that goes beyond individual advantage. In the third maxim, "think consistently at all times," the first two combine to form what Kant calls "reason."

I interpret this three-step process as developing the ability to bring together the cognitive and emotional-motivational processes involved in a coherent way. Initially it's irrelevant which parts of these processes the individual is conscious or unconscious of.

If we pursue the basic notion of integration, common sense provides a link between public spirit and the common good. While public spirit describes the motivational basis for a focus on the common good, common sense connects intention with reality. In this context it is important to link different points of view so as to come up with a pragmatically feasible solution that other people consider reasonable.

It is considered reasonable when the balance between individual and collective needs and expectations is maintained. It is unreasonable when no balance is reached and an approach to a solution conflicts with or deviates too widely from the knowledge and experience of a culture. If the common good is the goal, then common sense can act as a mediator of reason.

In this case common sense can be seen as the ability to intuitively recognize what is right and to do what is appropriate. This first of all concerns the subjective assessment of what is considered fair and just, but also beautiful and useful. It also includes the ability to recognize what is feasible in reality and what value conflicts can arise. In this respect, common sense is conservative because it excludes extreme or radical positions and aims to create balance.

Every realization of ideas of the common good requires common sense. On the one hand, common sense feeds the creative pragmatism needed to find practical approaches in controversial issues concerning the common good. On the other hand, the tension in ideas of the common good between the individual and collective satisfaction of needs is inherent in the concept of common sense: measuring one's own actions against how comprehensible they are to others. In light of the grand challenges we face today, one extension might be to expand the frame of reference and consider the effects from the perspective of the conditions of life on Earth as a whole. In this broader perspective of the common good, a decision should be acceptable not only to "the man on the Clapham omnibus" but also, for example, to "the tree on the side of the road" and "the artificial intelligence around the corner."

Isn't that yet another excessive demand? And how can common sense be developed first at the level of the individual? Finally, I would like to outline what the appropriate learning processes for an individual might look like.

III. COMMON SENSE IS FORMED BY EXPERIENCES

Simplification is a core factor in common sense. Its strength, but also its weakness, lies in the express integration of experiences. As meaningful as wisdom, humor, and natural wit may be, prejudices and stereotypes are equally dangerous. Common sense can mean different things depending on experience. "The doctrine of the mean" plays a different role for adolescents than for their parents or grandparents.

Practical wisdom as the highest level of common sense is the result of lifelong learning processes that no one can shorten or even skip. An assessment of what can be considered "normal common sense" requires inner maturity, which an individual has to develop through experience. Children and young people must first learn which rules and norms apply in the social environment. Their experience teaches them which intuitions they can and cannot rely on. This includes trusting other people as well as understanding the risks and dangers involved when dealing with the forces of nature, animals, objects, and the environment in general.

These learning processes continue into adulthood to the extent that new forms of self-reflection are developed when dealing with contradictory experiences. In the best case of a "common" sense, this leads to a more complex understanding of the world, in which previously conflicting perspectives lead to a new kind of simplicity on another level.

Theories of developmental psychology describe these processes as a higher level of experience, which can be described as inner maturity.[15] First of all, in adolescence we need to understand and accept the values and norms of our social environment. This also includes internalizing the experiences that make up the fund of common sense. As a result, we reach a provisionally stable state of adaptation to our social environment, which Robert Kegan calls the "socialized mind." This is the norm for many people and indeed remains so throughout their entire life. Others go a step further because in actively dealing with other people's various expectations they encounter conflicts that they cannot or do not want to resolve through further adaptation. This results in a reassessment of previous experiences and of course also to a relativization of one's own common sense. Suddenly what was previously considered common sense no longer seems helpful and even gets in the way. If we manage to arrive at our own convictions and truths, we have to defend them when they come into conflict with our environment. Choosing our own path means more inner independence and freedom, but also more vulnerability. Previous dependencies are not eliminated, but they now appear in a new light and can be reflected upon more consciously. Kegan calls this level of experience the "self-authoring mind." Some people are then able to take a further, final step in personality development. As a "self-transforming mind," they learn to locate their own truths in a wider context and do not have to insist on their truth. They begin to accept that simple truths are often unattainable and learn to tolerate contradictions and accept other world views.

It is immediately obvious that a common-sense saying such as "the jug goes to the well until it breaks" takes on new nuances of meaning at each level of experience as we gain more life experiences. As the wealth of experience grows, it then becomes possible to recall the experiential knowledge acquired in the learning processes outlined above and to apply it as common sense. In this way the individual's *sensus communis* becomes more effective.

This learning process in the development of common sense, from the intuitive adoption of experiences to practical wisdom, can be understood as the elaboration of a constant stream of new answers to the question of the relationship between self-determination and self-assertion on the one hand and, on the other, dependence on and being at the mercy of the other people.

CONCLUSION

The different aspects of the origin, function, and development of common sense, which we have discussed rudimentarily in this essay, suggest that we should not overburden the concept itself. A simple and above all open description is perhaps best suited to do justice to the rich history of the term. Common sense encompasses the analytically unfathomable ability of humans to orient themselves intuitively in their environment. This ranges from sensory-motor stimulus-response relationships to the highest cognitive achievements of practical wisdom. Common sense manifests itself in its own way at each of these different hierarchical levels.

The answer to the question posed at the beginning about the use of common sense in our era can be summed up as follows: Before we look for new perspectives, we should first make better use of the existing potential. This includes reinforcing trust in our own gut feeling, but also consciously practicing a change of perspective. It is about tapping into previously unused forms of knowledge and self-critically questioning established thought patterns. Developmental psychology suggests that common sense can be trained.

Those in particular who claim to have common sense should use it with caution. Generally speaking, this can apply to any of us! Common sense is not a universal weapon to be deployed when you don't know what to do next. But it is definitely a source of practical reason that makes an individual's inner voice heard and encourages us to trust our intuition. A hunch or inner conviction cannot replace a lack of factual knowledge, but it can close relevant gaps and guide our actions. Common sense shows its greatest strength when—often with humor— it brings overly rarefied ideas back to the human world of experience.

Common sense reaches its limits when it is no longer subject to scrutiny or wants to detach itself from focusing on the common good. It becomes even more difficult when common sense's power to simplify is abused in order to trivialize complex situations and mobilize the dark side of common sense (prejudices, stereotypes). We should therefore pay careful attention to how the idea of common sense is being used.

The most important extensions of common sense in the 21st century are likely to be in the areas that concern people's own power to act and their position in the world. The wealth of experience inherent to common sense should not stop at what "the man on the Clapham omnibus" considers reasonable and thus beneficial to the common good, but should also include the "tree by the side of the road" and the "artificial intelligence around the corner." In this way, it may be possible to develop one of the most interesting, but also most puzzling of human abilities in an evolutionary and meaningful way.

Notes

1. Sophia Rosenfeld, *Common Sense: A Political History* (Cambridge, MA/London: Harvard University Press, 2011).

2. Adam Smith, *The Theory of Moral Sentiments, The Glasgow Edition*, vol. 1 [1759] (Oxford: The Clarendon Press, 1976).

3. Thomas Reid, *An Inquiry into the Human Mind on the Principles of Common Sense* [1764] (Edinburgh: Edinburgh University Press, 2000).

4. Chris Moore, *The Development of Commonsense Psychology* (Psychology Press, 2013).

5. Hermann Haken, *Erfolgsgeheimnisse der Natur. Synergetik die Lehre vom Zusammenwirken* (Stuttgart: DVA, 1981).

6. For an overview, see Gerd Gigerenzer and Wolfgang Gaissmaier, "Heuristic Decision Making" in Annual Review of Psychology, 62 (1) (2011), pp. 451–82; and Daniel Kahneman, *Thinking, Fast and Slow* (New York: Farrar, Straus and Giroux, 2011).

7. Upon closer inspection, however, even the apparently simplest platitude often turns out to be a complex psychological effort when dealing with the world.

8. Emil Walter-Busch, *Common Sense und der Lauf der Dinge in Humanwissenschaften* (Paderborn: Brill Fink, 2023).

9. Ibid.

10. The tendency has been to emphasize the primacy of implicit assessment, which precedes conscious cognitive processes. See Timo Meynhardt, *Wertwissen: Was Organisationen wirklich bewegt* (Münster: Waxmann, 2004).

11. Timo Meynhardt, *Wertwissen*.

12. Helga Körver, *Common Sense: Die Entwicklung eines englischen Schlüsselwortes und seine Bedeutung für die englische Geistesgeschichte vornehmlich zur Zeit des Klassizismus und der Romantik* (Bonn: Rheinische Friedrich-Wilhelms-Universität, 1967).

13. Timo Meynhardt, *Wertwissen*.

14. Robert Nehring, *Kritik des Common Sense – Gesunder Menschenverstand, reflektierende Urteilskraft und Gemeinsinn – der Sensus communis bei Kant* (Berlin: Duncker & Humblot, 2010).

15. Robert Kegan, *The Evolving Self: Problem and Process in Human Development* (Cambridge, MA/London: Harvard University Press, 1982).

CHAPTER 12

BEYOND SEPARATION: WORKS BETWEEN CONTROL AND NON-CONTROL

HANS ULRICH OBRIST, TINO SEHGAL, AND PIET OUDOLF IN CONVERSATION

An edited transcript of the Convoco Art Conversation between Hans Ulrich Obrist, Tino Sehgal, and Piet Oudolf at the Convoco Forum on July 27, 2024, in Salzburg.

Hans Ulrich Obrist: I always remember the very first conversation Corinne Flick and I had when we met in London. It was about poetry. She told me about the idea of Convoco. It is now the 20th anniversary of Convoco, and as Convoco celebrates its anniversary,

I'm reminded of Roman Krznaric's insightful book *The Good Ancestor*,[1] in which he urges us to transcend short-term thinking. He tells us that we should find ways to go beyond short-termism, that our world is overly caught in the short-termism of deadlines and that we should think about more long-duration visions. I think this is precisely what Convoco embodies—the "longue durée," as Fernand Braudel would say. When Corinne introduced this year's theme, *How Can We Create a Free, Just, and Sustainable World?*, I immediately recalled a conversation I had with Piet Oudolf and Tino Sehgal for Piet's extraordinary book, published by Phaidon.[2] This conversation addressed the idea of a free, just, and sustainable world—of a *lebbare* world. The garden as a living organism is somehow the topic. And this brings us right away to our two speakers.

Piet is a visionary landscape and garden architect and designer who—together with his wife Anja—started initially in 1976 in Haarlem and then in Hummelo. Ever since he has developed very radical ideas about gardens and planting designs. What began as a nursery evolved into a radical, innovative approach. His gardens are among the most well-known. He is one of the key figures of the "new perennial movement" and has often worked with plant communities. This idea of a communion of plants, this idea of creating a relationship with one's surroundings, is something which is, as Piet says, not just about flowers. It's about seasonality. It's about spring, summer, fall. It's about decay, death, and decline, everything inclusive. In that sense, a successful garden is a balance between form and movement. It should seem natural and spontaneous, but never out of control.

And that brings us right away to Tino Sehgal, whose extraordinary work is also a negotiation between control and non-control. Tino creates constructed situations. It's an amazing invention of basically living artworks. Unlike traditional performances, his work doesn't rely on specific showtimes but rather, like a museum, has set hours. Tino's work is there from 10 a.m., when the museum or exhibition opens, until the evening. It's a living organism or, as he calls it, a constructed situation. Early on, he abandoned material production in favor of lived experience, and already at age of eleven, he decided to cancel Christmas, as an objection to the production of objects. This is of course a great anecdote in his biography. I believe that, like gardens, curating has the power to bring people together. It is also an important part of my work to bring people together. If we want to address the big themes of the 21st century, the challenge is that we need to go beyond the fear of bringing knowledge and the disciplines together.

In 2021, I was with Tino Sehgal in Blenheim Palace. It was an unforgettable experience, as Tino crafted a roaming choreography within the stunning gardens designed by Capability Brown.[3] Imagine visiting this magnificent park where individual works are transformed into dynamic scenes, allowing us to fully engage with these constructed situations. In the courtyard, you encountered a big group of people—actually interpreters of Tino's work—standing in two lines, facing each other, and humming. Then the humming stopped, and all of a sudden two of the protagonists stepped forward and started to sing. Yet Blenheim Palace also offered more intimate encounters. You had a situation where you could encounter Tino's iconic piece, *The Kiss*, on a marble floor. You were engaged in conversations in the rose garden, where you initially mistook the sound of humming for bees, only to realize it was human humming. It was a kind of *Gesamtkunstwerk*. And in this *Gesamtkunstwerk*, Tino shared his admiration for Piet Oudolf's work with me. This was about a week before I was recording the interview with Piet for the Phaidon book, so I invited Tino to join. It was fascinating to see that both Tino and Piet compose using people, and Piet, of course, composes with plants. This creates a profound connection between their work. I would like to begin by asking Tino to share his experience at Blenheim, and to tell us about his invention of a constructed situation.

Tino Sehgal: My work shouldn't be a mysterious thing; it's not about creating a mystery. Let me give you a little bit of background. I come from an uncultural family and grew up in an industrialized place in Germany, Böblingen Sindelfingen. I came to museums relatively late in life and soon realized that we are a society that believes the good life comes from producing things by transforming material and natural resources. Museums are temple-like buildings, the temples of these secular societies. The production of material goods was interesting to my father as an Indian immigrant because it was a measure of his success, but it was not so interesting to me anymore. Growing up in an environment where everybody focused on producing things, I became much more interested in the living—working with the living—and seeing how I can transform situations and people's interactions. Thanks to individuals like Hans Ulrich, I've now had a two decades' trajectory in the field of museums. Although I would say that I work with living material, or rather with living beings (humans), these places that initially felt a bit strange to me became my professional home.

When I discovered Piet's work—apart from really enjoying it as an aesthetic experience—I felt a kind of proximity. I thought, here's somebody who is working with other living beings, which are plants, and is constructing and composing with them in a visual way. At the end of the day, my works also have a visual component. When I was invited to Blenheim Palace, I wasn't really interested in something in the Palace, but I was interested in somebody like Capability Brown, who creates this combination of natural and artificial landscape, somebody who really composes with trees, with *Sichtachsen* [lines of sight], with perspective, and creates a connection between what he has composed and the environment around it. We are not thinking about conquering nature anymore, but more about living together in a way that is good for us.

HUO: When we talked about Piet's work and his interesting gardens, you also mentioned the connection of "going beyond separation." Separation is a sort of a fundamental defining feature of modernity, and you basically see it as an element of extractivist relationships with nature. Your work is about going beyond this separation. If you think about how to create this more free, just, and sustainable world, it means going beyond these separations. Can you talk about that a little bit?

TS: One way to see modernity, our current era, is as an experiment in separation, what happens when you separate things which usually belong together. You can see it, for example, in Western medicine—we take the body apart. You can see it in economics, in the division of labor. You can see it in wisdom, wisdom becomes academic disciplines. For every aspect of knowledge about life, we create an academic discipline. Or you can see it in ritual, what used to be ritual—like the Catholic Church—became different artistic disciplines. So, modernity is an experiment in separation, and I think that brought us a lot of benefits. For example, our era has the lowest child mortality rate than any other era or culture. But it also creates difficulties. As a social formation based on separation and specialization, we don't have an understanding of the whole anymore. That is what I was interested in.

HUO: And that's a wonderful segue, Piet, into your work. I am the Artistic Director of Serpentine Galleries in London. Every year, we commission an architectural pavilion. Rather than showing models of architecture, we build architecture because we believe that this is the way to experience it. This year it's Minsuk Cho, the South Korean architect. And the year Piet and I met, it was the Swiss architect, Peter Zumthor. He created a very beautiful and almost monastic space in Kensington Gardens. He said: "You've got to find me a landscape architect." So we brought Piet together with Peter Zumthor. In one of our first meetings, Piet told us that it's not about separated plants but about the togetherness of constructing. English gardens were initially a big inspiration for you, but you wanted to free yourself from that. You started to use more native plants in gardens. You were interested in doing that in your nursery and created a completely different model. Please tell us a little bit about your life with plants.

Piet Oudolf: I grew up in a family that ran restaurants and bars. We had no connection with plants. But when I got older—in my twenties—I began thinking about the rest of my life and I started to work at nurseries and got involved with plants. It didn't take long for me to realize that this was a field I could truly engage with. I had a sort of connection with plants, became very passionate about them, and started to travel to gardens, especially English gardens. I found myself healthily obsessed with plants. I wanted to do something with plants and so we started a small studio for garden design in the city of Haarlem and I went back to school to study plants and plant techniques, and we built gardens. We worked for a few years and became rather well known for our use of plants. However, we did not have enough space and decided to move to another part of the Netherlands. We started a farm where we could grow plants to use for our designs. That meant a big change in my life. We had no clients. The only thing we could do was work hard and build up the nursery to bring people in to buy the plants that we loved. We had a special nursery with plants that were not commonly found elsewhere, which helped us establish a distinct reputation. We traveled to England and introduced plants to the Netherlands, and we traveled to Europe and collected plants at nurseries. By doing that, we became a hub for people from England for the plants that we collected from the rest of Europe, and we became a hub for Germany and other countries for plants from England. We had a big network of growers in England and Europe who we exchanged plants with. We built up our nursery but didn't design any more. It took us six years to renovate the farmhouse, build up the nursery and a regular clientele so that we could earn a living. At the same time, we created borders, planting areas where we made examples so that people could see how we put the plants together. We met people from the "wild plant world," people who liked it that we introduced plants from the wild that we saw as having a potential for gardens. Plants that looked wild but behaved well and could be used in our planting. We created a community of people who came from the wild plant world and who came from the garden world. I would say that the garden world in the 1980s was all about decorative gardens, putting plants in the garden, waiting for the flowers, and then cutting them back. There was no seasonality and not the life that I thought we could put in the garden. I was looking for more spontaneity by putting other plants in the garden, like grasses—nobody did that back then—and I just put them in the middle and tried to compose gardens with them. I taught myself to design plantings by putting them together and being very critical of my own work. I built up a sort of knowledge of how to compose gardens because I had a lot of books about garden design, but they didn't really tell me anything. They were about complicated planting schemes. I had to learn it myself, and by doing that I got my first commission for a private garden. I think it was in 1986, 1987. And then, there was a publisher who came to us and said: "Do you want to make a book about the plants you're selling, because these are plants that people don't know." This was our first book which was called *Dream Plants for the Natural Garden*. It included pictures and descriptions. I did it with one of my friends who was a good writer. It took one year, but soon we attracted more and more people and magazines seeking fresh ideas and inspiration. They came to us because our approach was totally different. I felt confident in my approach, believing that the plants I worked with were a means of self-expression. That's why I kept going and was not afraid to do gardens in my own way. I didn't even ask people whether they liked it or not if it worked for myself and my friends. One of the key points of our work was that we shared everything we had. Sharing the knowledge and everything else made it a lot easier for me when I came to other people and asked for something—they couldn't say no. That's how we made things work in the 1980s and 1990s. After the book was published, I got my first commission in Sweden where I went to a conference about plants and public space. Public space is an area where a lot of work is done that you don't see. However, there's hardly any expression of green. One of the directors of a city near Stockholm asked me to do a garden at the library, which became my first public work. Before that, I primarily worked for private clients. When I started to work in public, I noticed that it was a chance to communicate with a wider audience, with more people than just a family.

HUO: There are many examples of your work: your Menorca Garden, your Somerset Garden, of course, the High Line, the Vitra Garden or the Calder Garden, which you're currently working on. In your gardens, the grasses are often very tall. They can be taller than us, two or three meters high. You compare them to dancers. You basically say, it's like a stage play.

PO: Between 20 and 40 percent of the vegetation in the world is more or less grass. Grasses are a very big thing in planting, and I thought about creating more movement and a sort of naturalistic idea. When you enter a garden, you see grasses and plants together, you think it looks wild. Well, it's not wild at all. It's organized and it's composed, and that is what I worked out more and more over all these years: how to create and plant things that give you the idea that you're in a natural habitat. That is why I like to work in public and in bigger cities where millions of people have no garden. You meet people and you engage with people so they become aware of things they would otherwise probably not have encountered. They sometimes never leave the city; they stay in the city. You connect people with something they probably have inside them but can never work out—only when they encounter it.

HUO: This idea of composing in time, Tino, is something you see in a way related to your work. Can you somehow react to what Piet was saying and link it back?

TS: One thing which attracted me to museums, although they were strange to me, was that they're one of the very few institutions that provide a perspective across generations. In museums, we think in centuries, and whatever I could criticize about museums and their kind of celebration of material artefacts and industrial culture, I had to acknowledge that they are some of the few institutions that really deal with long-term value creation and are not stuck in short-termism. It's our job as artists to define what is different in the 21st century as opposed to the 20th and the 19th centuries. I think the 19th and 20th centuries were a kind of juvenile moment of humankind where—like a teenager—we thought that we are so amazing and can dominate everything around us and that whatever we create is going to be better than what already organically exists on this planet. I think this kind of hubris is receding. Now we understand that most living things are more complex than what we can create. But how can we, as creative makers, put ourselves in perspective in relation to other living things and not just dominate them, as we did to a great extent in the

Western tradition? We fell a tree, ergo it's no longer alive and from the wood we make a sculpture. Even if that's still resource-friendly, it's the same basic kind of operating system as industrial society. Now, also as societies we are thinking more about trying to work with the living, for example with the re-greening of cities—and this is the approach that I see with Piet and myself. I don't think it's correct to say we dominate nature, we rather transform it. And that's what I see in Piet's work, but maybe also in mine: there's a kind of letting go, but there's also composition and control. That's why I feel close to your procedures. When you say it's like compositions, like an orchestra, but at some point also a living entity. You know what it is going to do, but not fully. You have to let it go its own way while still setting some rules and regulations. I think that is theoretically, philosophically, politically, more a relationship at *Augenhöhe* [on an equal footing]. Artistic work using technology or dead materials is all well and good, but I'm not sure it's helping us a lot to understand who we are in the 21st century.

PO: My work with perennials is very ephemeral. It can live for twenty years and then it's gone. I think everything we do is just temporary, and—if you look over time—even a tree is. Trees are sort of the skeleton of the gardens, especially in bigger places. You can make a woodland, you can make a meadow, you have different concepts to create a sort of movement. I think with perennials and grasses you create something very quick, very dynamic and changing. And the changing of this planting is what you experience as four-dimensional. Normally you don't have that in art. A garden grows and you cannot keep it as it is. It will grow into something else. For example, some plants will try to take over. In all my work we need people with a lot of knowledge to take care of it. If I look back at gardens that were made twenty years ago and their design and I look at the garden now, because of the people that take care of it, it's not a design anymore, but it's now even more beautiful because it has grown together, it's more organic. It fits. It looks like every plant feels happy with its neighbor. That is what we strive for, to make gardens that feel good, that make people feel good emotionally and create in you a state of mind that you want to return to. I think gardens are a good example, because if you're there in May and you come back in August, it's a totally different world. I think trees are good for later when the garden isn't there anymore, then the trees take over and they can carry on for a hundred or more years. In this way you take care of the future, but it is a whole process of thinking, how do you do that? This looks so simple on paper but it's more than just putting plans together. It's something that you're always thinking about. What will it do later? How will it end up?

HUO: It's fascinating, because when we invite artists to make a project, often they would rather like to do a garden. It happened last year: we invited Alexandra Daisy Ginsberg, and she said that rather than making an exhibition she'd like to create a pollinator garden in Kensington Gardens, a garden that would mainly be for pollinators but that we too can enjoy. Tino talked about it: there's a strong kind of move towards the idea of artists being interested in living organisms. What is also interesting in terms of statistics is—Piet, you said this in an interview—that a younger genera- tion, people between twenty-five and forty, forty-five, are the biggest group to take an interest in gardens. We observe the same in terms of art exhibitions. Shows about AI and video games and shows about gardens attract new audiences. This brings us to the future. Piet, you said that gardens are a promise to the future and that one has to guide people to that future. Can you talk about this idea?

PO: A garden is always a promise because you put something down that people don't really see. They see the labor and they see what it costs, and maybe in three, four months' time they see something happening. Of course, the whole process can be interesting for the person but the whole reason is that by making a garden you also introduce life. You introduce insects, but you also introduce creatures that you don't want: slugs, snails, and mice. A good garden has everything—the things you don't like as well. That's fascinating. Our garden was underwater for two and a half months, we lost twenty-four species in the front garden and still the garden looks good, but now I also know what a rain garden is. If your garden is underwater in the winter, you learn a lot. In that sense, it's a never-ending story of learning. This is also fascinating. It's like science: if you want to know more, you learn by doing. I think that is gardening, although it looks nice, it's not at all about flowers. In fact, it is, but not only flowers.

HUO: In conclusion, I want to talk about healing. This idea of healing is so important, and of course in Germany there was Hildegard von Bingen who worked a lot with plants and talked a lot about the healing qualities of gardens. And, Piet, you are also into that. You worked on a hospital project in Denmark. If we think of Hildegard von Bingen, we of course also think about music and sound. We began with Blenheim and the humming, the sound in Tino's garden. As many of us will experience music here in Salzburg, I wanted to end the conversation with a last question to Tino. We talked about this idea of how things that are not material can still transcend to many generations. Poetry is a case in point. Something immaterial can develop a strong multi-generational dimension. Like music, for example. Quite recently you did an amazing piece about Beethoven for the Kunsthistorisches Museum in Vienna, so I wanted to end with you telling us about this.

TS: I think the idea that material persists is relatively new. If we look back at antiquity and Plato, the thought was that ideas persist. With Whitehead,[4] we have this beautiful sentence describing the adventures of ideas, that ideas have their own life. When I was asked by the Kunsthistorisches Museum in Vienna to do something for the 250th anniversary of Beethoven, I thought how some of these tunes really had an adventurous life of their own. For example, in Japan there's a big cultural focus on the Ninth Symphony where hundreds of people come together and sing it. I was interested in why these melodies have their own life. I made a piece where these Beethoven symphonies are sung, and at the same time one body part moves. For the Fifth Symphony, you have the hand moving, or for the Egmont Overture it is just a choreography for the head.

To quickly come to the mobile phone childhood, what is true about plants and healing, especially about music and Hildegard von Bingen who worked with both of these modalities, is that we are in a vibration. We are in a vibrational, or energetic, or resonant exchange with a plant, with other humans and with music. When children spend time on their phone, they're not actually in resonance and that's a problem. Children don't learn interpersonal skills and that it is important to be in resonance. If we create a world that's too technological, we create blockages for resonance. We need to understand these vibrational exchanges and actively create them. Every social exchange apparently extends your life by seven seconds. I overheard this the other day, so I don't know the scientific source, but it made sense to me.

HUO: That's also a wonderful conclusion. Thank you so much, Piet. Thank you so much, Tino.

Notes

1. Roman Krznaric, *The Good Ancestor: How to Think Long Term in a Short-Term World* (London: W.H. Allen, 2020).

2. Cassian Schmidt, Noel Kingsbury, and Hans Ulrich Obrist, *Piet Oudolf at Work* (New York: Phaidon, 2023).

3. Lancelot "Capability" Brown (1716–1783) was the most influential and famous British landscape architect of the 18th century. Having worked on hundreds of parks and gardens, he developed the world-famous, natural-looking English landscape.

4. Alfred North Whitehead (1861–1947) was a British philosopher and mathematician.

CONTRIBUTORS

Prof. Gabriel Felbermayr, Ph.D. is Director of the Austrian Institute of Economic Research (WIFO) and a Professor at the Vienna University of Economics and Business. After studying economics and trade at the University of Linz, he went to Florence to pursue his doctoral studies. From 2004 to 2005, he was an Associate Consultant with McKinsey & Co. in Vienna. From 2005 to 2008, he was Assistant Professor at the University of Tübingen. From 2009 to 2010, he held a Chair in International Economics at the University of Hohenheim (Stuttgart). From 2010 to 2019, he led the ifo Center for International Economics at the University of Munich, where he also served as Professor of International Economics. From 2019 to September 2021, he was President of the Kiel Institute for the World Economy. At the same time, he held a Chair in Economics and Economic Policy at Kiel

University (CAU). Gabriel Felbermayr is a member of the Scientific Advisory Board of the German Federal Ministry for Economic Affairs and Climate Action, and the Chairman of the Statistics Council at Statistics Austria. He is Associate Editor at the *European Economic Review*. Gabriel Felbermayr's research focuses on issues of international trade theory and policy, labor market research, European economic integration, and current economic policy issues. He has published a large number of papers in international scholarly journals, policy briefs, and newspapers. His research has been recognized with various awards.

Prof. Dr. Corinne Michaela Flick studied both law and literature, taking American studies as her subsidiary, at Ludwig Maximilian University, Munich. She gained her Dr. Phil. in 1989. She has worked as in-house lawyer for Bertelsmann Buch AG and Amazon.com. In 1998 she became General Partner in Vivil GmbH und Co. KG, Offenburg. She is Founder and Chair of the Convoco Foundation. As Editor of Convoco! Editions she has published among others: *Is the Open Society Sustainable in Case of Emergency* (2024), *Equality in an Unequal World* (2023), *How much Freedom must we Forgo to be Free?* (2022), *New Global Alliances: Institutions, Alignments and Legitimacy in the Contemporary*

World (2021), *The Standing of Europe in the New Imperial World Order* (2020), *The Multiple Futures of Capitalism* (Convoco! Editions, 2019), *The Common Good in the 21st Century* (2018), *Authority in Transformation* (2017), *Power and its Paradoxes* (2016), *To Do or Not To Do—Inaction as a Form of Action* (2015), *Dealing with Downturns: Strategies in Uncertain Times* (2014). She was awarded the 2023 Prize for Understanding and Tolerance by the Jewish Museum Berlin. Since October 2023, she has been Honorary Visiting Professor and Professorial Fellow of the Humanities Research Institute at the University of Buckingham.

Prof. Dr. Dr. h.c. Clemens Fuest (b. 1968) is President of the ifo Institute–Leibniz Institute for Economic Research at the University of Munich e.V., Executive Director of CESifo GmbH, Professor of Economics and Public Finance at Ludwig Maximilian University, Munich, and Director of the Center for Economic Studies (CES) at LMU. He is among other posts a member of the Advisory Board to the German Federal Ministry of Finance, the European Academy of Sciences and Arts, the Scientific Advisory Board of the Market Economy Foundation (Kronberger Kreis), and the Foundation for Family Businesses in Germany and Europe.

Previously, he was President of the IIPF (International Institute of Public Finance e.V.) from 2018 to 2021 and member of the Franco-German Board of Economic Experts from 2019 to 2022. In 2013 he received the Gustav Stolper Award of the Verein für Socialpolitik (Social Policies Society, VfS), in 2019 he received the 2018 Hanns Martin Schleyer Award, and in 2023 he was awarded the Bavarian Maximilian Order for Science and Art. In 2017 Clemens Fuest received an honorary doctorate from the Karlsruhe Institute of Technology (KIT).

His research areas are economic and financial policy, international taxation, tax policy, and European integration. Before his appointment at Munich, he was a professor at the Universities of Cologne (2001–08), Oxford (2008–13), and Mannheim (2013–16). He is the author of a number of books and has published many commentaries and byline articles on contemporary questions of economic policy in national and international journals. He also writes for newspapers such as *Handelsblatt, Frankfurter Allgemeine Zeitung, Die Zeit, Süddeutsche Zeitung, WirtschaftsWoche, Financial Times,* and *The Wall Street Journal.*

Prof. Dr. Dr. h.c. Birke Häcker has been Schlegel Chair in Civil Law, Common Law, and Comparative

Law, and Director of the Institute of International and Comparative Private Law at the University of Bonn since 2023. Prior to taking up her position, she was, inter alia, a Fellow of All Souls College, Oxford, from 2001 to 2008 and from 2011 to 2016; from 2011 to 2016 a Senior Research Fellow at the Max Planck Institute for Tax Law and Public Finance in Munich; in 2016 she took up the Statutory Chair in Comparative Law at the University of Oxford and Professorial Fellow at Brasenose College; and from 2018 to 2022 she was Director of Oxford's Institute of European and Comparative Law. As an undergraduate, she obtained a dual legal education, reading jurisprudence at Oxford as well as German law at the Universities of Tübingen and Bonn. Her Oxford D.Phil. was in comparative private law. She publishes on a broad range of topics in English and German private law, comparative law, and legal history.

Prof. Dr. Stefan Korioth gained his doctorate in law in 1990 and completed his postdoctoral qualification in public and constitutional law. From 1996 to 2000 he was Professor of Public Law, Constitutional History, and Theory of Government at the University of Greifswald. In 2000 he accepted the Chair of Public and Ecclesiastical Law at Ludwig Maximilian University,

Munich. His publications include *Integration und Bundesstaat* (1990), *Der Finanzausgleich zwischen Bund und Ländern* (1997), *Grundzüge des Staatskirchenrechts* (with B. Jean d'Heur, 2000), *Das Bundesverfassungsgericht* (with Klaus Schlaich, 12th edition, 2021), *Staatsrecht I* (6th edition, 2022), and *Deutsche Verfassungsgeschichte* (2023).

Prof. Dr. Martin Korte, born in 1964, is Director of the Zoological Institute and Head of the Cellular Neurobiology Department at the TU Braunschweig. He also heads the Neuroinflammation and Neurodegeneration Working Group at the Helmholtz Center for Infection Research in Braunschweig. Among other things, he is a member of the Berlin-Brandenburg Academy of Sciences (BBAW) where he is also an elected board member. He was a founding member of Die Junge Akademie at the Leopoldina and the BBAW. He received the Ars Legendi Faculty Prize for innovative teaching in 2015 and the North German Science Prize (2nd place) in 2022. His research areas are the neural basis of learning and forgetting. Before his appointment to Braunschweig, he was a working group leader at the Max Planck Institute of Neurobiology in Martinsried near Munich and completed his postdoctoral qualification at the LMU

Munich. He is the author of several books. His latest books, *Frisch im Kopf* (2023) and *Gute Idee* (2024), were published by DVA.

Prof. Dr. Christine Langenfeld studied law from 1980 to 1986 in Trier, Dijon (France), and Mainz. She passed the First State Examination in 1986 and the Second State Examination in 1991. In 1989 she received her doctorate from Johannes Gutenberg University in Mainz. From 1991 to 1997 she worked as a research associate at the Max Planck Institute for Comparative Public Law and International Law and completed her postdoctoral qualification in 2000 in Saarbrücken. Since 2000 Christine Langenfeld has been a Professor of Public Law at the University of Göttingen. From 2008 to 2010 she served as Dean of the Faculty of Law. Since 2012 she has been Director of the Institute for Public Law/Department of Constitutional Law in Göttingen. From 2012 to 2016 she was Chair of the Expert Council on Integration and Migration. She is Chair of the German Section of the International Commission of Jurists, a member of the Board of Trustees of the Wissenschaftskolleg in Berlin, a member of the Senate of the Austrian Academy of Sciences, and, since 2016, a Justice of the Federal Constitutional Court (Second Senate).

Dr. Hans-Dieter Lucas is the Ambassador of the Federal Republic of Germany to Italy and to the Republic of San Marino. Before assuming his current post Dr. Lucas served as German Ambassador to France and Monaco (2020–23). From 2015 to 2020 he was Germany's Permanent Representative to the North Atlantic Council (NATO). From 2011 to 2015 he was the Political Director of the Federal Foreign Office, following two postings as the Commissioner for Eastern Europe, the Caucasus and Central Asia (2006–10) and Representative to the Political and Security Committee of the European Union (2010–11). Dr. Lucas has held various other positions in the Federal Chancellery, the Federal Foreign Office, and the German embassies in Moscow and Washington, D.C. He studied history, political science, law, and Catholic theology in Bonn and Paris and holds a Ph.D. from Bonn University. For his service he has, among other things, been awarded Grand Cross 1st Class of the Order of Merit of the Federal Republic of Germany and named as a Knight of the Legion of Honor of the French Republic.

Prof. Dr. Timo Meynhardt holds the Dr. Arend Oetker Chair of Business Psychology and Leadership at the HHL Leipzig Graduate School of Management. He is

Managing Director of the Center for Leadership and Values in Society at the University of St. Gallen, where he obtained his doctorate and postdoctoral qualification in business administration. For several years, he was Practice Expert at McKinsey & Company. Timo Meynhardt's work focuses on public value management and leadership, combining psychology and business management in his research and teaching. He is co-developer of the Leipzig Leadership Model and co-publisher of the *Public Value Atlas* for Switzerland and Germany, which aims at making transparent the social benefits of companies and organizations (www.gemeinwohlatlas.de; www.gemeinwohl.ch). His Public Value Scorecard provides a management tool to measure and analyze the creation of public value. He is also Co-founder and Jury Member of the Public Value Awards for Startups.

Hans Ulrich Obrist (b. 1968, Zurich, Switzerland) is Artistic Director of the Serpentine in London and Senior Advisor at LUMA Arles. Prior to this, he was Curator of the Musée d'Art Moderne de la Ville de Paris. Since his first show "World Soup (The Kitchen Show)" in 1991, he has curated more than 350 exhibitions. His recent shows include "Enzo Mari" at Triennale Milano (2020) and "WORLDBUILDING" at Centre Pompidou Metz (2023) and Julia Stoschek Collection Düsseldorf (2022). In 2011 Obrist received the CCS Bard Award for Curatorial Excellence, and in 2015 he was awarded the International Folkwang Prize, and most recently he was honored by the Appraisers Association of America with the 2018 Award for Excellence in the Arts. Obrist's recent publications include *Ways of Curating* (2015), *The Age of Earthquakes* (2015), *Lives of the Artists, Lives of Architects* (2015), *The Extreme Self: Age of You* (2021), *140 Ideas for Planet Earth* (2021), *Edouard Glissant: Archipelago* (2021), *James Lovelock: Ever Gaia* (2023) *Remember to Dream* (2023), and *Une vie in Progress* (2023).

Piet Oudolf, born in Haarlem in 1944, is a visionary garden architect and landscape designer and a key figure of the New Perennial Movement. He started his landscape and garden design practice with his wife Anja in 1976 in Haarlem and moved to Hummelo in the eastern part of the Netherlands in 1982 to start a nursery growing rare perennials. Some of his most famous works include the High Line in New York, the Vitra Campus Garden in Weil am Rhein (Germany), and the Hauser & Wirth Somerset Garden (England). His work has been featured in a number of publications, the most recent being *Piet Oudolf at Work* by

Cassian Schmidt, Noel Kingsbury, and Hans Ulrich Obrist published with Phaidon.

Prof. Dr. Philipp Pattberg is Director of the Amsterdam Sustainability Institute and Full Professor of Transnational Environmental Governance and Policy at the Faculty of Science, Vrije Universiteit Amsterdam. His current research analyzes options for institutional innovations to accelerate the transition to sustainability. His latest book is *Rethinking Climate Change* (forthcoming).

Prof. Dr. Moritz Schularick is President of the Kiel Institute for the World Economy and Professor of Economics at Sciences Po, Paris. He is an elected member of the Academy of Sciences of Berlin. In 2015/16 he held the Alfred Grosser Chair at Sciences Po. Previously, he taught at the Free University of Berlin, and was a Visiting Professor at the University of Cambridge. He is one of the recipients of the 2022 Leibniz Prize. In 2018 he received the Gossen Prize of the German Economic Association. He is a Fellow of the Institute for New Economic Thinking and a Managing Editor of Europe's most important policy journal, *Economic Policy*, a joint initiative between Sciences Po, CEPR, and CESIfo. He is a frequent consultant to central banks and contributes to public debates across different media. His research spans macroeconomics, finance, international economics, and economic history and has been published in *American Economic Review*, *Quarterly Journal of Economics*, *Review of Economic Studies*, *Journal of Political Economy*, *Journal of Monetary Economics*, *Journal of International Economics*, and several other journals. His research is supported by major grants from the European Research Council, the German Research Foundation (DFG), and the Institute for New Economic Thinking.

Tino Sehgal, born in 1976, is an artist. He lives and works in Berlin.

Prof. Dr. Claudia Wiesner is Professor of Political Science at Fulda University of Applied Sciences, a member of the Board of Directors at the Point Alpha Research Institute, and Adjunct Professor in Political Science at Jyväskylä University (Finland). She has been a Visiting Fellow at institutions such as the Minda de Gunzburg Center for European Studies at Harvard University, New York University, the Robert Schumann Centre for Advanced Studies at the European University Institute (EUI), and the Berlin Social Sciences Centre (WZB). Prof. Wiesner's main research focuses on Europe in the world and the comparative study of democracy and governance in the EU, putting particular emphasis on the related concepts, ideas, and theories. She is the Principal Investigator of the Jean Monnet Network "Debating Europe" and of the international projects "Transnational Governance and Human Rights" and "Practising Transnational Politics." Moreover, she chairs the ECPR Standing Group "Political Concepts." She has published with publishers such as Palgrave Macmillan, Routledge, Springer, and Nomos and journal special issues and articles in journals such as *Contemporary Political Theory, Journal of European Integration, Leviathan, Politics and Governance, Politische Vierteljahresschrift, Redescriptions, Parliaments, Estates and Representation, Zeitschrift für Vergleichende Politikwissenschaft*, and *Zeitschrift für Politikwissenschaft*. Her most recent books are *Politicisation, Democratisation and Identity Formation in the EU* (Routledge, 2024) and *The War Against Ukraine and the EU: Facing New Realities* (Palgrave Macmillan, 2024, eds. Claudia Wiesner and Michèle Knodt).

IS THE OPEN SOCIETY SUSTAINABLE IN CASE OF EMERGENCY? *2024*

ISBN: 978-1-9163673-8-8

With contributions by: Marietta Auer, Tim Crane, Gabriel Felbermayr, Clemens Fuest, Adrian Ghenie, Birke Häcker, Peter M. Huber, Stefan Korioth, Martin Korte, Jörn Leonhard, Timo Meynhardt, Hans Ulrich Obrist, Monika Schnitzer, Wolfgang Schön, Moritz Schularick, Claudia Wiesner

EQUALITY IN AN UNEQUAL WORLD *2023*

ISBN: 978-1-9163673-6-4

With contributions by: Marietta Auer, Paul Collier, Gabriel Felbermayr, Francisco H. G. Ferreira, Clemens Fuest, Raji Jayaraman, Francis Kéré, Kai A. Konrad, Stefan Korioth, Jörn Leonhard, Timo Meynhardt, Hans Ulrich Obrist, Christoph G. Paulus, Mathias Risse, Wolfgang Schön, Claudia Wiesner, Jonathan Wolff

**HOW MUCH FREEDOM MUST WE FORGO
TO BE FREE?** *2022*

ISBN: 978-1-9163673-4-0

*With contributions by: Bazon Brock, Tim Crane, Gabriel
Felbermayr, Clemens Fuest, Birke Häcker, Martha Jungwirth,
Bruno Kahl, Stefan Korioth, Jörn Leonhard, Rudolf
Mellinghoff, Timo Meynhardt, Hans Ulrich Obrist, Philipp
Pattberg, Herbert A. Reitsamer, Monika Schnitzer, Sven
Simon, Claudia Wiesner, Peter Wittig, Hildegard Wortmann*

**NEW GLOBAL ALLIANCES: INSTITUTIONS,
ALIGNMENTS AND LEGITIMACY IN THE
CONTEMPORARY WORLD** *2021*
ISBN: 978-1-9163673-2-6

**THE STANDING OF EUROPE IN THE NEW
IMPERIAL WORLD ORDER** *2020*
ISBN: 978-1-9163673-0-2

THE MULTIPLE FUTURES OF CAPITALISM *2019*
ISBN: 978-0-9931953-8-9

THE COMMON GOOD IN THE 21st CENTURY *2018*
ISBN: 978-0-9931953-6-5

AUTHORITY IN TRANSFORMATION *2017*

ISBN: 978-0-9931953-4-1

POWER AND ITS PARADOXES *2016*

ISBN: 978-0-9931953-2-7

TO DO OR NOT TO DO—INACTION AS A FORM OF ACTION *2015*

ISBN: 978-0-9931953-0-3

DEALING WITH DOWNTURNS: STRATEGIES IN UNCERTAIN TIMES *2014*

ISBN: 978-0-9572958-8-9

COLLECTIVE LAW-BREAKING—A THREAT TO LIBERTY *2013*

ISBN: 978-0-9572958-5-8

WHO OWNS THE WORLD'S KNOWLEDGE? *2012*

ISBN: 978-0-9572958-0-3

CAN'T PAY, WON'T PAY? SOVEREIGN DEBT AND THE CHALLENGE OF GROWTH IN EUROPE *2011*

ISBN: 978-0-9572958-3-4

www.ingramcontent.com/pod-product-compliance
Lightning Source LLC
Chambersburg PA
CBHW071535200326
41519CB00021BB/6498